Brian's Guide To Manifesting An Awesome Life

By

Rhiannon Faulkner

*Copyright 2020. Rhiannon Faulkner.
All rights reserved.
www.briancopthorne.com*

When People Say,
How are You?
Enough with the line
I am fine.
In order to help you heal
You need to voice how you really feel.
As you already know,
Anxiety and depression
Make you feel incredibly low

This book is dedicated to Daniel,

May it always be your reminder of how utterly awesome the world can be if you believe in yourself.

Although I may be short, I am your biggest fan.

Each time you say I can't,

I will be there to say Oi Dan,

Yes, you damn well can.

Love Brian.

Introduction

Firstly, I want to thank you for buying this book. You had loads to choose from on the shelf, that show you how to manifest the masses into your life, yet you chose mine. If you are familiar with me and my way of teaching, you will have made a fairly good assumption that this one ain't the easy route. And for that I applaud you. If someone bought it for you, they must think highly of you and want to help. However, don't worry if you choose to chuck it in the bin, they will never know. But there's no harm in seeing what they were so excited about to share with you is there?

Manifesting anything into your life is possible as you are about to find out. In fact, you already manifest without realizing it daily as I will show you in this book. We are going to master the art of working together with your guides and the universe to be able to lead an utterly awesome, happy abundant life.

Sound good? Is that what you came for? Wanting to know how to get the universe to bring you what you want, need and desire? Then let us begin by starting with you.

The content of this book has been rolled out on an online 4 week course for the last 6 months before she would even consider writing this for me, with Mrs. F hosting live videos daily to a group of beautiful souls wanting to change their lives.

It was a painful, heartbreaking eye opener for every single one of them including Mrs. F herself, as they realised how they'd all been withholding miracles and pure joy for years, by being their own worst enemy.

Amazing results began to show themselves in the first few days for many, and by the end of the 4 weeks, a new way of life was being enjoyed by all who had completed the course intently.

People saw drastic changes in their health, wealth and happiness. Their success was well deserved, and no one is happier to see them enjoy their newfound way of life than their guides and me.

So now I want to help you, the reader. Nothing happens accidentally. You are reading this for a reason. All I need from you is a promise you will do everything I ask you to in this book, in the order it is written. I need you to keep going even when it gets so god damn painful you want to screw the book up and fling it across the room, or leave it for another day that we both know won't ever come.

I need you to invest in you.

You have already paid for the book, so why not get your money's worth and actually do what it asks you to do?

Brian's Guide to Manifesting an Awesome Life.

CHAPTER ONE:

Understanding Your body

You are first and foremost a wonderful, perfect beautiful loving soul, living in a human physical body. Your body has housed you for your entire life so far very well because you are still alive and kicking. It responds to how you treat it. Obvious when we talk about diet, healthy living and exercise, as we all know full well by now that if you eat well, your body has more energy and your skin looks great, same as if you exercise your body looks toned compared to if you don't exercise.

But did you know that your physical body is made up of energy centers called chakras, throughout your body that need to spin healthily for your body to fully function and keep you healthy?

Did you know that an emotional problem you hold onto over time, if not sorted, can prevent this chakra from spinning properly?

The first lesson of the day is to remember that every physical problem stems from an emotional one.

Let us park that for a minute, but we will come back to it throughout this book…and let us first look at the chakras and how they relate to your body.

Brian's Guide to Manifesting an Awesome Life.

We start with what is called the Root Chakra, which is situated in your groin and glows a beautiful deep red colour when spinning healthily. It is responsible for your sense of belonging, your purpose in life and that amazing sense of loving life and wanting to succeed. It houses your ability to become financially abundant, creative and gives you that passion and zest for living life to the full. Goals, dreams and ideas are created here.

A little higher up, just about where your tummy button sits, is your sacral chakra that glows a divine orange colour when it spins healthily. This one is all about happiness and quite simply giving you that feeling of being content and sublimely happy in all you do. When this one is healthily spinning, you can look forward and aim for goals with passion in everything you do. Compassion for other people and being able to see their side of things also stems from this chakra, which is important to help you not take personally other people's actions or unkind words.

Then we come to the solar plexus chakra that is seen as a bright gorgeous yellow colour and is situated in your gut, under the ribs. This is responsible for giving you that inner knowing when something is right or wrong, whether you should or should not do something or trust someone. It's amazing, a guiding force that is built into your human body. It churns when something is not quite right, it makes you think, it makes you question people, places, choices.... when it spins healthily of course. It is that one chakra that it is responsible for all

Brian's Guide to Manifesting an Awesome Life.

those times you proclaim, "I KNEW that was going to happen !!"

The chakra that often ends up being the problem with a lot of people is the big 'ole heart chakra, which when healthy, shines a gorgeous combination of green and pink as it spins in the core of your chest. It is the love center and easily stops spinning properly when you get hurt. Negative experiences in the area of love such as jealousy, envy, grief, anger, rejection and so on all have a huge impact on this vital chakra. Every experience in love and relationships, right from early days with parents, friends and partners are designed to help you grow as a soul and understand the wonderful emotion called Love. Preventing yourself from receiving love because of a painful experience before, is more damaging than you realise. Love is a big deal and will be the focus throughout this journey to manifesting a happy life. Sit tight, you got this!

Next up is the throat chakra. When this is stopped from spinning beautifully shining its incredible off the scale blue / aqua colour, you lose your voice and ability to speak your truth. When it is healthy and working well, you are not afraid to voice your fears and concerns, to speak loudly and proudly proclaiming to the world who you are and what you stand for.

Brian's Guide to Manifesting an Awesome Life.

The third eye which is very much thought of as the main chakra that you use to "be intuitive" or psychic, is seen as a magnificent purple colour when the chakra is clear and healthy. It is responsible for your knowledge and intuition. This is where you receive the vision and clarity of what the outcome of a situation or decision will be. Your "foresight" comes from your forehead! Who would have thunk it!

And lastly, right at the top of your head, in fact it hovers just above your head, is the crown chakra. This is a beautiful sensational white colour when it is open and spinning healthily.

It is where your guidance comes from, it is where you connect to the universe and are shown the potential in all you do, including day to day decisions and for life in general. This must be open to receive in order to see the magic and awesomeness that is accessible to you in this life you lead. It is quite literally where the answers come from up above.

Interesting blah blah you may say, but what has this got to do with manifesting?

Well, firstly I would like you to remember the line from earlier on.

"Every physical illness stems from an emotional problem"

If your chakras are not spinning healthily or not being used to their full potential, your body starts to

Brian's Guide to Manifesting an Awesome Life.

show you where it needs the help to be fully functioning again. Because, see, your body operates on an energetic level as well as physically and emotionally. And your human physical body is a channel for the universe to connect to and work through. To shine its awesomeness through. Every single one of you. You have been made that way. You've always been able to work perfectly well with every sense that your body has, but over time, life may have got to you, other people may have got to you, other people's beliefs may have kind of got in the way; and you've begun to shut down a little or even a lot and ended up in a royal mess. **Feeling** your way through life is how you started off as a young child. Remember the **feeling** of utter excitement and joy you had when your birthday was coming up? Or Christmas eve and just **knowing** that there was going to be a present under the tree for you? Remember when your favourite relative would pay a visit when you were tiny, and you felt such a warm loving exciting glow when they hugged you? Remember when you were little and you decided that when you grew up you were going to be an astronaut or a deep sea diver and you **believed** it and felt so happy excited and confident that you would achieve your dreams. Do you remember your imagination being so vivid that you could not quite understand why the adult could not see what you did? The excitement and happiness and joy that you felt when you did whatever you felt like without a care in the world?

Brian's Guide to Manifesting an Awesome Life.

And then life happened. People voiced their opinions about your choices. You were told don't do that; you look silly. Other children laughed at you saying you were going to be a deep-sea diver when you didn't even have your gold swimming badge. Your dad had an issue with your favourite relative, and they never turned up to your house anymore. They stopped coming and you felt sad but covered it up because you didn't want to go against dad.

You stopped dancing or singing because it was deemed uncool by the group of kids who never talked to you or let you play with them on the other side of the playground, just in case they laughed at you again. You began to find a way to fit in with other people and not proudly stand out as your unique wonderful awesome self. Maybe your parents had a different plan for you and wanted you to be a ballerina instead of a truck driver or maybe, just maybe, your parents weren't able to support you in looking forward because of their own life choices. Or maybe they did have the money and wanted to invest in the best education ever for you and encouraged you to take a different path, because they didn't have that chance themselves as a child and feel they missed out.

Adulthood brought bills, responsibilities and decisions that took you away from following your happiness and joy. Having children made you prioritise their needs over your own, you made admirable sacrifices in order to give your children the best possible life you could imagine for them. You made a decision to

Brian's Guide to Manifesting an Awesome Life.

just keep doing any old job that paid enough money even though you hate it, you hate the people you work with and its so far away from your dream job it's like being on another planet, but hey, bills…..

Some of you are even stuck in a relationship because it is the right thing to do for other people. Kids would be affected if you chose happiness over commitment, you would risk having the kids taken out of your life if you left, your family would hate you for your selfish decision, or maybe you worry that your partner wouldn't be able to cope without you so hey, keep on keeping on….

Fear of running out of money has kept you from living for the moment. Maybe a relationship that ended left you in turmoil, unable to see how you could start all over again without feeling drained and tired. Maybe you have decided it is too late, you have missed your chance. So now its surviving that is important. Keeping afloat.

So, it is really simple to diagnose the area of the problem in one of two ways just by looking and listening to your body.

Firstly, what colour are you currently drawn to wearing now? Because you will see that it always matches the colour of the chakra that needs your attention. Blue? your throat chakra is screaming for your attention; you are not speaking your truth. Red? Focus on your root chakra and I bet you struggle right now to feel happy with your life and sense of belonging in the

Brian's Guide to Manifesting an Awesome Life.

world. Yellow? Are you constantly second-guessing things and doubting your gut feeling? Are you riddled with anxiety and have that stomach in knots kind of feeling?

What if you just wear black every day? That does not match a chakra you tell me. Nope, indeed it does not, but what it does tell me is you are trying to cover up your shining light and hide yourself away, so you will not be noticed. I still see you. You need to give this book a chance and by the end of it I will have you happily wearing white!

Secondly, list down your physical ailments. What part of your body is beginning to show signs of neglect and emotional issues? Because each chakra directly affects the organs and parts of the body that it sits by. Constant urine infections? Heavy periods? Bowel problems such as IBS? Then you will be glad to know the first chakra we are going to be working on is the root chakra. Teeth problems? Are you angry and suppressing your true feelings for fear of annoying someone else? That is an area of the body that the throat chakra is responsible for. Also, sore throats, is a common sign that this chakra needs working on.

Have a think of all the physical symptoms you suffer with daily and relate it to the relevant chakra that controls that part of the body. It can lead to a "Doh!" moment but also make you realise how awesome your

Brian's Guide to Manifesting an Awesome Life.

physical body is as its been trying to show you what it needs to heal itself for quite some time.

Some of you are living with some life changing illnesses and have had to adapt your way of life to accommodate the illness or dis-ease. COPD, asthma and pleurisy are all stemming from the heart chakra being unable to function properly. Do you have heartache? Do you like yourself as a person? Do you feel unloved? Or worse, do you feel unlovable? Or has that one person's hurtful assumption of you from years ago stuck with and you have told yourself you are better off without love ever again?

So, what about the sticky out bits of my body? I hear you ask. Well, this will be a mind- blowing realization for you when I tell you that arms lead from the heart, and the left arm is all about receiving love while the right arm is about giving love. Hmmmm, starting to understand why your left shoulder gives you problems now, or the root cause of the trapped nerve down the right arm? To heal, you need to see your problem with giving and receiving love.

The legs are leading you forward in life, and stem from the root chakra where your sense of belonging and purpose in life is created. Are you walking in the right direction through life or are you on the wrong path? How do your legs feel? Achy, tired, swollen?

Is the knee or the ankle the problem area for you? Does it give you trouble? Are you refusing to bend

Brian's Guide to Manifesting an Awesome Life.

and go with the flow in life? Or are you stubborn and determined to keep going forward even if it makes you depressed?

Foot problems say you are not happy with where you stand in life right now.

Who has skin problems? Eczema, psoriasis or sore red patches literally say you are unhappy being in your skin. You are unhappy being you.

Do you have weight issues that you cannot shift no matter what diet you try? Excess weight my darlings is a result of you trying to hide yourself away. Why are you hiding your beautiful light? Why are you hiding away from the world? Let us work on finding your fabulous spirit again and help you to shine it wherever you go without dieting. Yes, without dieting.

So to be able to channel or allow the beautiful energy of the universe to flow through you and bring you all the abundance and wonderful things you desire, we must first work on becoming a clear channel. By removing the blocks of negative emotion that you have built up over years of hurt, trying to change who you are, how you are seen by the world and self-loathing, we can begin to reconnect you positively to the universe.

Are you ready? Are you ready to receive the love that the universe has been so desperate to bring, but you have denied yourself? Are you ready to enjoy all the

Brian's Guide to Manifesting an Awesome Life.

wonderful experiences and riches of this material world on earth that you thought were just for a select few?

Let us begin. All I ask is that you do this properly, in full, one chapter at a time and in order. Even when it gets hard, personal, painful and downright nasty. No skipping of the mundane, boring or physical aspects and no ignoring the emotional stuff you have stored deep down for your whole adult life.

Let's unscrew you. Because I want to help you have an awesome life as I can see you are worthy. It is just you who can't see that right now.

Brian's Guide to Manifesting an Awesome Life.

Chapter Two:

The Root Chakra

The first chakra is the Root chakra at the base of your spine, or groin area. This is where we need to begin.

The moment you are born into this world, your soul secures itself or roots itself to this chakra, like a click and clunk motion. It ensures you are safely strapped into the human body ready for the ride of your life this time round. You are excited, filled with enthusiasm and zest for life, ready to experience life at 100mph with a smile on your face.

This chakra is responsible for your **purpose in life**, your **sense of belonging** and your **creative** abilities. (Those of you that stopped there and said that you are not creative, please know I am not just talking crocheting or knitting, bear with me)

Having a purpose in life is easy when you are young. You have no responsibility therefore you can just get on with seeing that every day is a learning day. You have parents or carers to be able to sweat the big stuff for you and you don't even see half the stuff that has been done to provide the food on the table or the petrol in the car to be able to get to the play café. You just focus on the fun and *JOY* in your day. If you do not like

Brian's Guide to Manifesting an Awesome Life.

something, you don't do it. You make choices going by the way it makes you *FEEL*. Did it feel good, did it taste good, if yes, you did it again, if not, you didn't. Life was an amazing exciting adventure that you got to repeat every day you woke up.

You have one sole/soul purpose in life and that is to simply *en-JOY*. But now as an adult, life does not feel so exciting. You wake up with anxiety, worrying about the day ahead, the bills to pay, the money in the bank account and your relationship with another human being. How did that happen?

The answer to that is over time, your anxiety crept in, you felt inadequate, silly, wrong, fearful, not good enough, because of observing other people's reactions towards you. As a child, you heard the adults in your life worry, you learnt about their opinions based on their life's experiences, good and bad. You realised you had choices in this life and you were allowed to air on the side of caution, you were able to decide what advice you took from other people in your life, good or bad.

You did not like the feeling of anxiety that you had when something didn't feel right. You didn't like the feeling of embarrassment you had when your friends mocked the bright coloured knee high socks you wore as a child, so you chose to wear white ankle socks to fit right in with them. You liked the feeling of being accepted by the crowd on the school playground, even if it meant you had to hide your love of quirkiness.

Brian's Guide to Manifesting an Awesome Life.

You began to realise at school age that your family life behind closed doors was different to your friends. You then began to question if yours was right or wrong, but soon clicked on that being different did not always make friends. So, for an easier, quieter life, you learned how to adapt to your new circle of friends and changed.

Falling in love felt good, but having to learn to change yet again, or maybe go along with the other persons beliefs became necessary to keep the relationship feeling good. Responsibility of caring for someone and thinking of their needs as well as yours meant, that sometimes it was easier to just keep the peace and agree with your boyfriend or girlfriend through fear of an argument or losing them. Because the bonus of being in a relationship meant that you were loved, safe and had someone to help you steer your way through life. Even if it was just surviving instead of being blissfully happy. How the hell did that happen? When did you become the person who would put up with second best? You used to fly through life as a carefree soul excited at every new opportunity. And now…

So now I must tell you that your purpose in life is simple. To find and *feel* the ***JOY*** in your life. That is, it. Do not complicate it, just re read that one sentence over and over until you ***FEEL*** the excitement and relief. Easy! You can do that! ***FIND. AND. FEEL. THE. JOY. IN. EVERY. AREA. OF .YOUR .LIFE.***

Brian's Guide to Manifesting an Awesome Life.

A **sense of belonging** is the second thing that is housed in the root chakra. Some people have that security ripped away from them at an incredibly young age, with trauma happening in the early years to their safe secure family unit. But most people at the very least know where they belong. You have a family name, a group of people who are in your life every day, be them parents, siblings or friends. So, at a young age, you know that you belong somewhere.

But as you age, you become aware that even the people you love the most in life are different, unique, their goals, plans, beliefs, even religion, differing from yours. You begin to search to see where you fit in. You search for others who are like you, who might accept you or you try and change and fit in to conform with society.

All the while, experiencing feelings of loneliness, solitude, failure and disappointment.

But when you were tiny, that sense of belonging came naturally, from accepting without judgement the life you had and the experiences you enjoyed each day. You confidently chose not to do something. You boldly announced you did not like something and refused to do it. Until the parent in your life told you that you must eat your broccoli as it will make you big and strong, but the smarties were bad for you and you couldn't go outside without clothes on, because , well, err… other people…..

Brian's Guide to Manifesting an Awesome Life.

Nothing better than watching a young boy drop his jaw and point furiously at a sports car driving past him in all its glory and declare that when he is big, he is going to have a red one of those. Nothing sadder than to see the adult tell him he has got no hope in hell, does he realise how much money that thing costs and besides, it is a gas guzzler too which is frowned upon. The lesson unwittingly learnt there was oooh I LOVE that car, but it is not good and does not make mummy happy.

So, I ask you a question, that may take you time to answer fully. Grab a pen and paper, you may want to do some working out…

Who has your power my friend? Let me help you work out who exactly has it….

Do you live life to the full every day without a care in the world and without a thought as to what other people would think of you or your actions?

NO? Then who has an influence over your decisions?

It could be your parents.

Brian you say, they are amazing people and have sacrificed absolutely all their wildest dreams for me to be able to have an education, a good upbringing and a car for my 17th birthday. I cannot jack my job in as a doctor after all I have cost them. It was their dream to

Brian's Guide to Manifesting an Awesome Life.

see me graduate and bring good standing to our family name. Even though I am not happy, I cannot blame them.

This is not a blame game. I just asked who has your power. Who do you think you are living your life for?

It could be your children.

Brian for goodness sake, my kids are my world. I give them everything, heck I would give them the clothes off my back if they needed it. They certainly do not have my power; I CHOOSE to do everything I do for them.

True that. You are an amazing giving person and an awesome selfless parent. But you bought this book because the title said "How to manifest an awesome life" so you must feel like something is missing.

But do you go without all the time for your children? Why do you not lead by example and show them that everyone is worthy of being happy and receiving things? Could you not give yourself a treat each week that is just for you and you only? How often do you do that? Do you have time for just you? Or have you sacrificed the salsa class you dream of because that money could be better spent on the children? What are you frightened of? Your children thinking you are a bad parent because you make time for yourself?

Brian's Guide to Manifesting an Awesome Life.

It could be your friends.

Do you feel unworthy or not good enough with your friends? Do you have to try and fit in to the group, is there someone who makes you aware of your imperfections? Do you choose what part of your life you share with them or do you hide some parts of your belief system just in case it upsets the apple cart so to speak.

Do you have different friends for different occasions? Friends who you know you can open to and other friends who you dress up for, clean the house before they arrive and slap some makeup or deodorant on for?

Digging deeper now, hold on tight….

It could be a PAST relationship that has your power.

The ex-partner from ten years ago who really was not any good for you but thank goodness they are gone now: however, do their cruel words still influence your current relationships? Remember when you were mocked for being too fat or too thin, for being too ugly

Brian's Guide to Manifesting an Awesome Life.

for them or too loud? Are you completely natural without a care in the world in your current relationship?

There is the first ouch, plenty more to come I am afraid.

It could be your ex-boss.

The boss from the last job who made your life utter hell and passed you up for promotion because he said you just did not cut the mustard without any further explanation…. Is he the driving force behind you still to this day in your current job, the voice in your head that says you are going to fail, no matter how hard you try? Is he the reason you beat yourself up and analyse every step you take or is he the reason you are defensive and angry when people judge your performance?

Is it an experience that has your power?

Has there been a time when someone was very cruel to you with their words or actions and you live in fear of feeling like they made you feel again? Do you find yourself changing or hiding your true self, or hopes and fears just in case it may happen again, even if that person isn't in your life anymore?

Brian's Guide to Manifesting an Awesome Life.

Does an illness have your power?

Maybe you think that you cannot live the life you love anymore because you got sick and now your abilities are limited. What if a doctor with lots of super qualifications after his name has declared your diagnosis means that you are now on a downward decline and can only hope to manage life instead of live it to the full? Is the illness the reason why you limit your way of life in case it causes more complications or problems?

Does society have your power?

Being different to the image that your society or media currently say is perfect, is a real battle for many of you, especially the younger generation. Being able to connect with celebrities and perfect airbrushed faces sure does make a lot of you feel inadequate. Your common sense goes out the window and you forget that the person doesn't even look like that in real life but technology, computers and editors have created a picture to entice you to buy the product or lifestyle the celebrity is paid to sell. You believe that you are substandard, and you begin to hate what you see in the mirror.

Filters on Instagram, Facebook and Snapchat make you look the same as societies idea of perfection, yet it also highlights how far from this look you are naturally. This makes some of you hide your incredible natural light forever more, through fear of being less

Brian's Guide to Manifesting an Awesome Life.

than perfect. It leads to self-loathing which is so terribly sad to watch from here.

Maybe you are a keen sports person. You have enjoyed the sport your entire life, becoming successful over time but you are still not blissfully happy with your life. How could this be? asks the entire nation watching. Maybe the pressure of pleasing all the people around you to continue winning is a little too much and has zapped the fun out of it, maybe the pressure of failure is all too real now, as it means letting others down. When did your life playing a sport become less about the sport and the *feeling* of *JOY* you had and more about pleasing others?

Maybe your sexual preferences do not fit in with your family's religion, beliefs, expectations and oh my, the list is endless isn't it? But the bottom line is, you are living your life as society wants you to. So, society has your power.

So being able to be honest with yourself about why you do or do not do certain things in life is a huge important first step to being able to lead a life of awesomeness. Please do not write down why you do these things, just answer my question – who has your power.

Now re read your list of who has your power in your life. Sit still, close your eyes and imagine a huge pair of scissors cutting pieces of rope to those people or situations or memories from the past, and see the rope falling away from your body.

Brian's Guide to Manifesting an Awesome Life.

    Do it again, go round your entire body snipping away at all the cords from top to bottom, from your head to your toes, making sure no rope is restraining you anymore. Get faster, get more confident, get snip happy, making sure not a single thread is left. *SEE* in your mind's eye all the rope on the floor and watch yourself step over it and walk away. Freely. Breathe my friend, breathe. Did you feel relief? Excitement? Freedom? Smile, that was the first step to you leading an awesome life. Do not worry or think about the ifs and buts, just pat yourself on the back as you just did something amazing for yourself. You set yourself free, from the restraints you kept yourself in.

    So, when the root chakra is not working properly you will be experiencing some unpleasant health issues in the groin / pelvis area. Take a moment to acknowledge how your body has been affected physically by this chakra stopping spinning. Things such as IBS, UTI's, Prostate problems and bloating. Cervical issues too for women are of course covered by this one. Aches and pains in your hips and backbone when you do the simplest of things should also be noted. Remember this chakra is responsible for everything in this important area.

Brian's Guide to Manifesting an Awesome Life.

CHAPTER THREE:

Setting Your Intention

Now we have recognized who or what had our power, we need to focus on your purpose in life. It is easier than you think, it is not a goal to achieve something or to become someone or something. It is to **'feel' JOY** and **HAPPINESS** in everything you do. That is, it.

Sit comfortably and tell me what emotion is missing from your life that you so miss. It could be love, happiness, joy, peace or even contentment.

Do not attach it with having someone or something in your life. Another person cannot bring you that inner feeling you so crave and miss. It comes from within and we are on the road to finding it again. The truth is when you look back at happier times in your life, your body felt that incredible emotion by itself, another person did not. They may be associated with that happy memory but your own being created and allowed the positive emotion to engulf your being. If your word you are using here is LOVE, then focus on the memory of how it physically feels to be in love. Am I right in saying your body tingled, your heart missed a beat and pumped at double the speed of light? You felt warm inside and sublimely alive!

Be careful not to focus on the object of your love or heart's desire, as that is not the emotion itself.

Brian's Guide to Manifesting an Awesome Life.

So, I want you to decide on your word and sit comfortably with your eyes closed. Imagine the top of your head opening like a sliding door and take some deep breaths. There is a waterfall of pure golden light directly above your head, like someone has turned a tap on and it is flowing down, filling your head with the light. **FEE**L the warmth, the heat, **SEE** the golden light fill every part of your body, as it runs like a river through your physical body, touching every single part as it goes. It goes down your neck, rushing down your spine, expanding through your entire torso, touching every organ as it goes. It flows down both your arms, right down to your fingertips, making you tingle, and your hairs stand on end. Down down down the hips, the legs, filling your knees with the light and rushing down the shins, filling all your tiny toes with the divine golden energy and out into the ground.

Draw more and more of the never-ending flow of light from up above your head, this time watching and feeling the light fill each of your chakras, making them splash their colours throughout your body like a rainbow in the sunlight. White, Purple, Blue, Green, Pink, Yellow, Orange and Red. See and feel the light and the chakra colours flow out of your physical body filling the room you are sitting in with the divine colours.

Let us go again, this time as the beautiful golden energy enters our head from up above, put the word that

Brian's Guide to Manifesting an Awesome Life.

best describes the emotion you desire to feel again in your life. See it written in the waterfall of energy and watch it enter your head and travel down, down, down through the head, neck, body, down the spine, and watch that word lodge itself firmly into the core of your deep red root chakra. See and feel it lock itself in place. Whether your word is JOY, PEACE, LOVE, HAPPINESS or CONTENTMENT, it does not matter, just see your intention set in place.

Now open your eyes. Feel your root chakra glowing and spinning healthily with your word of intent deep inside. You should also be able to physically feel a warmth or heat now.

Getting Creative

Creativity is also an important function of the root chakra. When this chakra spins healthily, you can act on ideas and goals you have. Having a hobby or pastime is not just for fun, it helps your body function in an important way as a pure channel.

When you worry and let anxiety take over your mind, you are blocking your guidance and true potential in a situation because you are trying to control a situation all by yourself without channeling the universe. You end up blocking help by trying to solve a situation alone. You are effectively telling the universe that you do not

Brian's Guide to Manifesting an Awesome Life.

want the answers or solutions brought to you, but you would rather keep the problem.

Getting your creative abilities flowing naturally and freely is so vital, in order to be able to receive answers from the universe. You do not need to be sweating anything alone! So, taking up a hobby, focusing on something that brings you quite simply pleasure and joy for that moment in time is very productive. It does not matter whether its painting, drawing, DIY around the house, writing, gardening or cooking; while you're focusing your mind on something that is fun, the answers to your problems can come to you. Remember the word of intention that you just placed in your root chakra, is your sole purpose in life – and you are worthy of finding it in every single moment of the day! So, when you find yourself panicking, worrying and stressing you cannot possibly be enjoying it, so scrap that and go back to doing something that makes you feel good and happy!

When you worry about something that you really need to get sorted, like finding a better paid job, or a huge bill that has landed on your doormat, your energy of fear, worry, panic and failure stops the universe from being able to make itself heard. Remember that you are a channel for the universe to flow through and it needs you to be open ready to receive. The block that you are creating is simply a waste of time. Once you take your focus off the problem and instead give all your energy to something that is making you relaxed happy and

Brian's Guide to Manifesting an Awesome Life.

chuffed, you will receive the answers or solutions to your problems.

Think of this one simple rule, you get what you give energy to. Everything is measured in FEELINGS by the universe, so if you feel good you will receive more of it and if you feel anxious, you will receive more of that too. You are in control of letting the universe know what makes you happy, so make sure you tell them what you really want by feeling happy emotions. Plus, this makes your life much more manageable and fun don't you think? So, no time for worrying, instead you need to only allow what makes you feel good in your life. Leave the big stuff that needs sorting to the universe!

Sitting quietly, focusing on creating something is calming, good for the body and the soul, so physically and mentally you are benefiting. But the biggest benefit by far, is the universe can begin to work its magic for you.

Think of it as a child screaming for their dinner to be made and you need to entertain them while you prepare it for them. Giving them a colouring book to occupy them creates a calmer place for you to be able to focus on cooking the food. It is the same for the universe, they do not need to battle with you while you are quietly colouring.

A perfect example of this happening to a lady I know all too well, is she absolutely hated her day job and was becoming depressed and withdrawn by the day. She

Brian's Guide to Manifesting an Awesome Life.

was shutting down faster than an electric garage door until suddenly she stopped and declared she could not do it anymore. She simply stopped work. She knew she could not afford to stop working but she had also come to the breaking point that I am sure you all know too well. She stopped prioritizing the bills and for once she succumbed to the painful realization that she absolutely hated every part of her day. After a few days of hiding under the duvet and wallowing in her depression, she had the crazy ass idea "out of nowhere" (cough cough) of having a go at making cement garden gnomes. Much to her kid's horror, the kitchen became filled with upside down molds and grey little feet sticking out of them in every corner of the tiny kitchen. But the laughter was contagious. The determination to get it right took over and the stubbornness kicked in to get it right each time a concrete gnome broke before leaving the mold. She would start again and again, becoming obsessed to get it right until one day her kids came home to find about 25 grey perfect gnomes lined up along the kitchen counter. They asked her what on earth she was going to do with them, and she said she was now going to paint them. They could not get why she was doing this without an end result or logical reason, but she didn't have one to give them. She was almost obsessed by this point at watching these gnomes come alive.

    She spent days painting them, giving them bright vivid coloured hats and boots, trying out different colour combinations and even buying new paints. She then

Brian's Guide to Manifesting an Awesome Life.

proudly put them outside in her tiny garden and roared with laughter at the sight of them. They were adorable, she felt pride and pure joy at having made something for the first time so well.

It rained and they all got ruined, with the paint running down the side of their little faces. She scooped every single one of them up, dried them up and took them back inside to the kitchen table where she re painted them and then researched a good varnish that would withstand all weather.

One of the children logically suggested that she should sell them, and her business head went on and she agreed it may be fun. She signed up to craft fairs and along with the kids helping, she set up her stall alongside a lot of experienced crafters. The laughter that could be heard from behind the gnome stall was hilarious. This lady could not control her giggles as she saw herself selling gnomes that were bringing delight to other people. She found she was holding conversations about spirits such as fairies and gnomes and the elementals to all sorts of people and her laugh was contagious. People were asking big questions and she was thoroughly enjoying helping them,all the time spreading the joy with the help of a bunch of concrete gnomes that she had lovingly made.

Now when she did the math's, there was no way a profit was being made from this to even pay one of the household bills and so it was obvious that it

Brian's Guide to Manifesting an Awesome Life.

was not a replacement job. But this lady did not want to stop because she was being filled with so much joy over the last few weeks. She was sleeping better, waking up excited to start all over again, or to go buy a new colour paint she wanted to use for a gnome. She woke up with ideas and was jumping out of bed feeling positive for the first time in a long time.

When she thought about how she had coped without doing her regular job, she realized that enough money had arrived in her bank account without her having to source or earn it. A tax rebate had been given to her while she was busy using her creative flair and it had made sure all the bills had been paid. It was about time that she started earning though as it would not last forever. So, she asked herself what she wanted to do that would make her happy. The answer was to work with me to do what she loved best, to teach spiritualism. And that ladies and gentlemen, is how I got the battle axe Mrs. F to teach the online course that lead to this book.

Running the online course daily with live videos each day to a bunch of wonderful humans who were feeling the same as she had been, stuck and looking for answers, changed her way of working and living. Writing this book now and making my teachings available to you reading this brings her joy and satisfaction every day. She wakes with excitement every morning and sleeps well every night. And without realising it, she had replaced her income without ever making another concrete gnome again. They sit as a

Brian's Guide to Manifesting an Awesome Life.

constant reminder to her in her garden and all around the house, much to the annoyance of her son, that following what brings joy and happiness in life, allows new ideas to flow and doors to open in life. You have a choice whether to sit and refuse to move forward and stay depressed and unhappy punishing yourself, or to let go of the steering wheel and let the universe guide you to a new happy way of living.

So, what is your creative hobby that you have always wanted to try? Is it cooking or gardening? Anything that gets you to still your mind is what the universe wants you to focus on. Give us a helping hand here, we are ready to work with you. All we need you to do is still your mind, remove what you're worrying about just for a short while and focus on ***FEELING*** the *joy*.

Strip and strut

A really simple way to get the root chakra moving again is to walk. Would you believe it, something so easy and natural that you have been doing since a year old? I can hear you groaning from here, but bear with me, this will work sooner than you think.

You started off walking as an innocent child with enthusiasm, excitement and freely using every muscle

Brian's Guide to Manifesting an Awesome Life.

and bone in your body, to be able to get from one place to another. Now as an adult you, without realising it, put the focus on your legs being the only part of your anatomy that moves you forward. Now I need you to walk from the hips. Let the hips move first and the leg follows. Try it in the comfort of your own home and privacy before you go out in public, but very quickly you will see what I mean. It actually FEELS better, it is natural, and your hips were made to swing and sway. You do not need to over accentuate it, but just move with your hips first please. Then the legs follow, naturally and easily bending at the knee. Basically, you are being given permission to sway that butt like John Travolta and I know you can do it better than that guy. This is all helping the energy flow and giving the root chakra a literal shake to get it spinning healthily again.

    Feeling stupid? Then you need to re-read the section before this called Who has your power? Why are you caring what you look like to other people when your physical, mental and emotional health is paramount? Within a couple of days, you will find yourself walking properly again. All the years of holding yourself tight and restrained, feeling awkward as you walk past other people, hiding unknowingly who you are and dimming your beautiful light, has actually led to you walking stiffly and compensating for pain and dis-ease inside your body.

    Some of you are not too keen on exercising for many a valid reason. Some cant, because of illness or

Brian's Guide to Manifesting an Awesome Life.

pain. If this is you, whenever you do walk, albeit slowly just around the house, then please still do as I have described. You do not have to be out walking for miles. Even the steps you take around your daily routine will transform your chakras ability instantly. Those of you that have chest problems and breathing struggles, just begin with a few easy steps, shooting from the hip first.

Some of you are avid exercisers, participating in classes and workouts and even running long distances. I am still asking you to join us in this, it is a vital step towards your wellbeing and creating an awesome life.

Going for a ten-minute walk even just once a day will do so much good. Open up the top of your head as you walk and connect to the beautiful energy of the universe, see it flow through your body and fill and rejuvenate you as you take in all your surroundings outside. Become aware of the noises, traffic, people, birds, animals, nature. Keep pulling that light through your head and see it go right down to your toes as you walk. Breathe as fully as your body will allow you to and be proud of yourself. You are making a change already. You are giving yourself the love and attention you deserve.

As you gently strut your stuff, I want you to imagine and *SEE* in your mind's eye all the fog that has been building up around you over time fall to the ground. For the stubborn ones amongst you, ask the universe to strip it away. Depression, anxiety and

Brian's Guide to Manifesting an Awesome Life.

negative thoughts about yourself from years and years ago need to be cleared away. Ask the universe to help you clear it. Mrs. F likes to see it as sheets of wallpaper being stripped off from her head to her toes, and she steps over it as it hits the floor. Try it, and soon you will see how the world around you becomes literally insanely brighter with every step. This fog of depression and negativity has been smothering you, preventing you from seeing the awesome world of opportunities that are around you. It has stopped you from using all your senses such as smell and sight to their full capacity. The trees become greener, the grass too and the colour spectrum will look as if it is doubled for you before your eyes. Be prepared to keep stripping your wallpaper of fog for weeks and weeks, each time it gets less and easier to remove, but keep going until you do not feel the need to anymore. You are removing the exterior block between you and the universe and the outside world. No more hiding, it is your time to shine and receive!

    Before you know it, you will connect the walk with feeling better. If you miss a daily walk and strip and strut session, you will notice the frustration build up in you. This is your body communicating its needs in order to stay healthy on all levels. Listen to it, it really does know best what it needs.

Brian's Guide to Manifesting an Awesome Life.

To Do List

Set your intention / desired emotion in the root chakra

Work out who or what has your power

Cut the cords

Open up to connect to the universe

Think of a creative hobby to enjoy

Walk with the hips leading the way

Strip off the sheets of fog around you as you walk

Brian's Guide to Manifesting an Awesome Life.

CHAPTER FOUR:

Becoming Your Own Best Friend

Grab a mirror for me. Put the book down, I shall wait. Now take a close look at yourself in your mirror. Make eye contact with yourself for me. Struggling? Does that make you feel uncomfortable? Why? Don't you like what you see? Did you feel unhappy with what you see? Did you comment on how tired you looked, or older than you would like? Did you notice something that you are not happy with on your face, hair or skin?

Now focus on the eyes. Really focus on the eyes and stare deeply into them for me. The eyes are the window to the soul and staring right back at you is a reflection of the real you. The small child you once were is in there. As you look into your eyes, become aware of how you physically feel. I bet there is a sense of sadness beginning to creep in about now.

That person looking back at you in the mirror has been abused, berated, ridiculed and hated by you. That person looking back at you in the mirror has been told daily that they are not good enough, not beautiful enough, not clever enough, not nice enough, by you.

How many other people in your life do you say negative things to? Do you walk up to someone in the street and tell them they are too fat, too thin, too loud, too ugly, too annoying?

Brian's Guide to Manifesting an Awesome Life.

How many other people in your life do you make cover up their face with contouring foundation, so it looks more acceptable in the current fashion trends? Or suggest to them to just wear baggy clothes and explain to them that their second roll of skin on their tummy really shouldn't be seen? Have you ever told another person in your life that they will not ever make it because they just have not got what it takes before they have even tried? I do not suppose you have ever gone up to someone in your life and told them that they don't deserve love because they aren't simply good enough have you? Do you buy the favourite food for each of your family members in the weekly shop, but leave one person out as they just do not warrant the expense and make them eat what everyone else's choice is instead? I am guessing the answer was a no to all these questions, so here is a simple question for you my friend. Why do you tell that person in the mirror negative things like this on a daily basis?

That person in the mirror has stuck with you through everything so far. They have been rather good to you, silently battling on while you knock them down at every step, crushing their every decision and highlighting their failure.

Hold the gaze with your reflection and please make a promise. That you will from this day forward protect that person and look after their every need, the same way you do for a friend or child that you adore unconditionally. Promise them that you will from

Brian's Guide to Manifesting an Awesome Life.

this day on, stand up for them, support them, believe in them and LOVE them for even trying at life.

From now, you will stand in front of this person you see in the mirror and you will get in the way of negativity coming their way with every ounce of your strength and you will be their voice.

Keep looking into the eyes staring back at you and now ask out loud what you can do for your new best friend to help them be happy today. Ask them what they need, ask them what they are craving and ask them how you can help them today. Be prepared to let the emotion out that you are feeling inside right now. Crying is good for the mind, body and soul. It may be guilt you are feeling as you begin to connect with the child you once were, and you start to think of all the negative things you have told yourself over the years. You may feel a sense of loathing for the person you see and are not quite ready to accept what you are seeing and feeling. That is all ok, let us just agree to accept that today, we are going to move forward with the goal of becoming best friends with our-self. Think of it like the new kid that you have been assigned to look after on the first day in school. Even if you are embarrassed to be with them, you know you can be polite and compassionate if you try hard and help them find their way.

Put your hand on your sternum bone, which is in the center between your ribs and keep looking deep into your eyes in the mirror. Ask again, what you can do for

Brian's Guide to Manifesting an Awesome Life.

your friend that will help them right now. **FEEL** the answer through your hand. It may be a sense before an actual word, you may sense that they want to sleep, eat a particular food or listen to some music. Whatever it is, do it now. You would if it were a love interest or your child, so no questions asked, do what you **FEEL** your best friend needs. NOW.

It is time to get ***SELF-ish.***

A new part of your daily routine is to look into the mirror each morning and ask your reflection what they would like to do today. No negative excuses are allowed and no refusals. No compromising and no questioning. You are finally putting your own needs first.

If your new best friend wants to eat a tub of chocolate ice cream, then give it to them without the lecture of weight gain. You will make sure that they get to choose one special food item in the weekly food shop that is their absolute favourite, regardless of the fact no-one else will eat it. If your friend wants to sit on the couch and watch movies, then sit on that damn sofa for at least one movie today.

Take your new best friend on your daily walk, shooting from the hips John Travolta style. Let your best friend breathe in the fresh air and just BE with them. Give them water, sunshine and sleep just like you would any other living thing. I bet you look after your dog better than you have yourself before now!

Brian's Guide to Manifesting an Awesome Life.

Ask your friend what their favourite colour is, ask them what they find funny. Accept the answer as truth without telling them why they cannot admit to that in front of anyone else just in case someone else doesn't approve.

Focus on how you speak about your new best friend, as remember they always hear your opinion of them even when it is just a thought inside your mind!

Correct yourself when you catch yourself saying:

I am no good at that

I always suck at….

I hate my……

I can't…

I look awful in……

I am not good enough to……

I am not well enough to ……

I cannot afford that………

I don't have the time to…….

When you have a shower or a bath, take the time to pamper yourself. Do not just rush the process, give your body the attention it deserves. Let the water that your body needs to survive feed your skin as well as wash it. Take the time to wash your hair, condition it not

Brian's Guide to Manifesting an Awesome Life.

for looks but for what it needs to flourish. Notice bruises and scars and see what your body has been through. Recognize how strong your physical body is for still functioning the way it does even after everything it has been through. Take a moment to imagine what your body looks like inside underneath the skin. Hear your heart beat strongly, pumping the essential blood around to all the organs. Pretty incredible hey?

Do not punish yourself when you eat, thinking negative thoughts of how bad this is going to affect your physical shape or energy. Instead, eat what you are drawn to, as once you are paying attention to your body, it will be able to tell you what it needs to eat too. You will begin to find that you are craving different foods, maybe even ones that you have never tried, and you have no idea why. If you listen intuitively, with feeling and emotion, you will begin to realise that your taste buds tingle at the thought of a particular food that the body needs to heal itself. This is the bodies way of responding to the love and attention you are giving it. It is saying more please! Go with it, do not question it. Just do as your best friend asks.

Your role now as your own best friend is to stand up for you. When other people say negative things or ask something of you that you do not really want to do, your job is to say NO.

There are several ways of saying no politely but firmly. You do not ever have an issue saying no sod off

Brian's Guide to Manifesting an Awesome Life.

when someone else you love is being treated unfairly, so now do it for yourself too.

Have fun trying out different ways of saying the word NO.

NO.

Nope.

Nada.

Na-ah

Hell NO

NOOOOOO

There are more severe ways, but I cannot write them for fear of offending, but you know exactly which words I mean.

Do you feel lighter already? It really does not take long my friend. Keep going.

Ask your friend what they would like to wear today. What colour feels right? And do not cover up their beautiful face with slap. Show your friend that you love them au natural and that you are accepting them for exactly how they are.

Remember the word of intention, the emotion you desired in the last chapter that you placed in your root chakra? Please ask your-self what they think would

Brian's Guide to Manifesting an Awesome Life.

bring that emotion into their life right now, in this exact moment in time.

Is it cheese? Music? Swimming? What brings you a *feeling* of **JOY** or **LOVE** right now?

30 seconds of pure uninterrupted bliss can indeed be accomplished by eating a piece of your favourite food or a few minutes of listening to your favourite music. Not just any old music, but something that sings to your soul. You know, the music you used to listen to before it became old and uncool. What music used to get you dancing and bopping back in the day when you were a carefree child? That is the music I want you to play.

Did the cheese make you smile? Did the music make you laugh? Good, repeat this daily. If your friend wants smelly stinky cheese every day for the next month, your friend will get it.

I bet I am right when I say you do not spend nearly enough money on you. You ration yourself and put yourself at the end of the priority list. You would give another person money if they asked to borrow it without hesitation, yet you will not give yourself that same amount of money to blow on a pair of shoes without thinking twice. You would buy your children shoes and the special packet of cereal they begged for in the weekly shop, but you won't buy yourself the food that only you like to eat in the house. You have unknowingly punished yourself for a long long time and have treated yourself as a second-rate human being

Brian's Guide to Manifesting an Awesome Life.

compared to everyone else in your life. Think of this my friend; if you do not put yourself first, you will be no good to the people you want to be there for. You must get selfish. You must include yourself in the people you look after and love.

      The universe simply brings you what you think of. It brings you what you tell it with your thoughts, feelings and emotions, good or bad. So please for the love of cheese, start thinking and talking nicely about yourself. Otherwise the universe has no choice but to bring you more hardship.

      Repeat out loud to yourself each time you find negative thoughts about doing something or having something creep into your mind these three words

    I AM WORTHY.

    Because you are.

Brian's Guide to Manifesting an Awesome Life.

To Do List

Be nice to yourself

Check in with yourself every morning and ask what you need, then get it!

Protect yourself from all negative people and situations

Know your worth.

Start saying no.

Brian's Guide to Manifesting an Awesome Life.

CHAPTER FIVE:

The Sacral Chakra

This chakra is a game changer when you get it sorted. When it is spinning healthily you can feel real **Happiness**, have **Compassion** for others and feel true **Passion** for achieving your **Goals** in life.

It is a glorious orange colour and sits in your stomach, just about where the tummy button is. It affects vital organs such as the womb, intestines, reproductive organs and lower back. Do not forget the skin, muscles and bones in this area are also affected by an unhealthy chakra. Take a moment now to see how your physical health is here. A bloated tummy, IBS symptoms, dietary problems. Are you finding yourself having to change your diet to compensate for these issues? Are you attempting to cut out something such as gluten or fiber to try and ease it? First, let us get to the bottom of the emotional problem and let's see if we can improve your physical wellbeing by focusing on your emotional state first.

Happiness

Depression, anxiety and grief are the result of being unhappy. So many of you suffer with this on different levels at different stages of life. You always think it is a result of something happening to you, a situation, a circumstance. But I want you to think of it as

Brian's Guide to Manifesting an Awesome Life.

your reaction to something. It is an end result where you cannot see the way out of something. It is your reaction to change in your life when it was unexpected or not what you wanted to happen.

    These emotions are very real and can engulf your every thought. Remember in the last chapter, we spoke about stripping away the fog of depression that surrounds you, preventing the universe from being able to get through to you. Also remember that you get what you think of as the universe responds to whatever you put your energy to and brings you more tenfold.

    So instead of focusing on why you are feeling anxious or depressed, we now need to switch your focus to what you do want more of. So, this means that when you are worrying about not having enough money, you are putting all your energy on the fact that you don't have enough money, so you will get more to worry about, not having money. If you turn it on its head when you are stressed over your financial situation and begin to think about how good it feels to have money, you will get more of that exciting feeling you associate with having money. By having money! The universe does not send you lessons, it sends you what you want, and you tell it what you want by your FEELINGS.

    When you have a problem that is keeping you up at night, riddling your body with fear,panic and kick starting anxiety attacks, instead of feeding the fear by re playing the scenario and the what ifs and buts in your

Brian's Guide to Manifesting an Awesome Life.

mind trying to find a solution, simply begin to imagine as if you already have what it is you need. Your imagination is an incredible human ability that has a huge important role to play in manifesting as we will see further along this journey. Remember, I need you to do this book in order, with every step we cover being important, but for now, just imagining a happy outcome or solution to what you are worrying about is a really good start.

So now is the time to talk about how much you are loved and adored by the universe and your own personal guides, even if you don't know it and even if you don't yet love yourself as much as you should and soon will. You are a natural channel for the divine love up above, every single human being is, not just a chosen few. It is literally how you were made. Your soul is an extension of the universe, it is made of the same stuff that you are drawing down through your head. Pure, amazing, unconditional, love and divine light. It doesn't matter what you do, it still pours through you.....when you let it.

If you choose to shut down and prefer to try and deal with life and problems all by yourself, focusing on the fear and anxiety, your guides have to wait patiently until you ask for help and become open to the love and help.

So now, each time you feel fear and anxiety, I want you to ask for help. Even if you cannot yet see, hear or feel the universe and its helpers around you, just ask. Does not matter if you say it out loud or in your

Brian's Guide to Manifesting an Awesome Life.

head, you will be heard. Remember, the universe goes by how you **FEEL**, and this includes when you reach out for help and become ready to receive. But speak to the universe, become vocal and remove your pride and ego when you have a problem. Allow yourself to be helped. You do not need to be sweating anything alone.

Trust and faith are needed to be able to continue with your life **KNOWING** that your request was heard, and miracles are beginning to be manifested for you. Ask once with pure intent and forget it. By the way, you can even ask in a sassy arsey way, we don't care, as long as you ask for the help. See your guides like secretaries, stood by your side waiting for your instruction, holding a notepad and pen. You can ask them for small things and big things. Maybe you need to go out but at the same time you should stay in and wait for a parcel delivery. Ask that the parcel is delivered when you get back instead of while you are out. Maybe you are worried about being able to find a job urgently. So, ask for your next job to be brought to you in a way that you cannot possibly miss it. Then leave it and know it is being sorted.

Then, once you have offloaded your problems, you can begin to feel lighter and more positive. Now you can get back to your one purpose in life: feeling that emotion you set as your intention in your root chakra. You ask, leave it, get ready to receive.

Brian's Guide to Manifesting an Awesome Life.

Go busy yourself doing something that brings you no other end result other than **_JOY_**, eating the cheese, gardening, drawing or out for a simple strip and strut session! For the record, a lot of cheese was consumed while doing the online version of this book!

Ever heard of the phrase belly laugh? Does it make sense now that you see your happiness is an effect of a happy sacral chakra that is stored in your belly? Laughter, real belly laughing is so good for your soul and essential in keeping it healthy guys! Do not hold back on the giggles, laugh even if no one else does, laugh even if it is deemed untimely by other humans who have not sorted their stuff out yet. Laugh and see it as the best free medicine known to mankind. Once you remove the fear of someone else's thoughts towards you, or the thought of other people's opinions, I think you will be able to laugh more freely than ever before. Give it a try, realising that without the limitations you have allowed to restrict yourself in life, there are actually a hell of a lot of funny things and situations to be found everyday.

Compassion

What if it is another person that is causing you heartache and anxiety or depression? The sacral chakra is responsible for you being able to have true compassion for others. It may take a hell of a lot of cheese and gardening, but I assure you that you will get

Brian's Guide to Manifesting an Awesome Life.

this one eventually. Being able to **FEEL** real compassion for someone who has quite frankly been an ass to you, means you finally realise their problem has nothing to do with you personally. It is their problem and you are reacting to their action. You are not responsible for someone else's thoughts or actions and you cannot ever change another human being permanently. You are only ever responsible for and in control of yourself.

The saying you can only help those who want to be helped is important here. Keep in mind that on your quest to manifest an awesome life, you must become **SELF-ish**. So, let's just focus on what you can change, which is your reaction to the other persons action.

So, when someone is opinionated and judging toward you in a hurtful way, it creates fear, pain and anger in you. Fear and anger are both emotions that block you from being able to connect and channel the universe and its helpers, your guides. So instantly, you have allowed the other person to affect you in a big way. The usual reaction of justifying your side of things or arguing back telling them they are wrong or nasty, is a total waste of your energy. It achieves nothing at all except for more pain. The need to put them right in their way of thinking of you has become more important and your focus is on how or what they think of you. Stop.

Remember you are going to receive more of what you put your energy on, the universe must as that is the way it works. So, you will now receive more judgement

Brian's Guide to Manifesting an Awesome Life.

and hurt as you are effectively telling us that you want to experience more of it.

If instead, you open up and draw down the divine light from up above, the pure unconditional LOVE that flows for every living thing on the planet, you will instantly feel calm, see your worth and within a few moments, you will have INSIGHT as to where that angry person is actually coming from. You will have COMPASSION and understanding as to their point of view or what their real issue is. You will be able to see them reacting to life around them just like you do. It does not make their anger or outburst right, but it removes the need for you to wreck your beautiful channel with anger, fear and anxiety. So, bottom line is, it is all about you!

You will be able to send them love. The love that you are channeling. The energy of love that they need just like you to have a happy positive life. You will begin to see that every single person is on their own path with the same blocks that are preventing them from experiencing happiness.

You will be able to see it is not a race or a competition. You are not against each other. You are all on the same page. The day will come when someone cuts you up dangerously on the road and instead of shouting and beeping your car horn at them, you'll find yourself slowing down to make it easier for them to pass and you'll wonder what the hell has happened to you.

Brian's Guide to Manifesting an Awesome Life.

You grew, that is what happened. You now don't have to keep taking things personally.

Haaaaving said that.... please know that you absolutely do not have to let someone treat you badly at all. You can cut ties with them. In-fact you must, for your best friend you, to be able to **FEEL** happiness and contentment in life. But you won't feel guilt over cutting them out, either temporarily or permanently out of your awesome life.

So, what about the people that you cannot cut out of your life you may ask. Such as children, obnoxious demanding diva teenagers that you are absolutely devoted to, yet who are sucking the life out of you emotionally. Or parents who have raised you their entire life and given you the best they could to enable you to have a head start in life and now still act as if they can tell you what to do even though you're an adult.... Well, once you have sussed the ability to include yourself in your list of people that you love unconditionally, you will find yourself being able to voice your truth and set boundaries so that their demands are not killing your soul slowly.

Personal responsibility comes in here along with compassion for the other persons point of view. Recognising that if you have been one of those parents who always caved in and gave the child whatever they wanted to keep the peace, through fear of a confrontation, it will be difficult and a new experience

Brian's Guide to Manifesting an Awesome Life.

for the now teenager if you suddenly begin to say no to them. They need time to accept the change of rules. You need to see that they are now growing and learning about their own personal responsibility. You are helping your children grow by showing them that you are important too and are included in the pecking order. It is not all about them. They now have to go through the process the same as you are right now, seeing that anger doesn't get them anywhere and compassion for another person is the way forward. The sooner they feel gratitude towards you as a parent and for everything you have done for them, the sooner they will become a happier soul.

Now turn that around and what if it is the parent that can't let go of how life was. Parents who are demanding and causing you utter guilt for living your life your way and not their way.

Maybe they expect you to take a path that you just don't want to and now you are an adult you are torn between upsetting your parents and being true to yourself.

So how do you have compassion for a controlling parent.... by seeing things from their point of view and recognising how difficult it must be for their life to suddenly change. They have devoted every single penny of their life to you, they did not have to, they chose to with love. Maybe becoming a parent gave them something wonderful to focus on and a chance to forget their own misgivings and concentrate on your life

Brian's Guide to Manifesting an Awesome Life.

instead. Maybe that was easier for them, than to sort their own issues out as a young adult. Now you have grown up, you leave and what do they focus on now? Who can they love unconditionally and prioritise if you are not there anymore?

Begin to see your parents as people, not just parents who have shouted the orders all your life. See them as souls just like you and once upon a time they had dreams and goals just too. But they are pretty awesome already, as it turns out, they changed their plans to make room for you. Their love for you was so strong, they did the best job they knew how to give you an awesome life. Even if you don't agree with the way they did that, I think the best gift you can give them as a form of gratitude, is to help them see you are grateful, respectful and have compassion for their feeling of emptiness now. You can help them to lead a fulfilling life prioritizing finding their own *JOY* and happiness. The ability to have compassion for their situation and feeling of loss and fear of change, will help your relationship take on a whole new level of friendship.

Some parents may have your cases packed on your 18th birthday and holding the one-way ticket to Las Vegas that they have been waiting for your whole lifetime. If you feel rejection or anger at their ability to plan their own life, you need to remind yourself that you are an individual adult and responsible for your own choices. What we really need to focus on is the fear you have of beginning the next chapter in your life being in

Brian's Guide to Manifesting an Awesome Life.

control of making your own choices. Anger and blame towards your parents for not supporting you financially anymore, need to be replaced with excitement of planning your future.

So, in a nutshell, stop taking everything that has happened to you so personally. As it turns out, it was not aimed at you at all, everyone in your life has their own fears and battles that they are trying to overcome. Realising that other people have their own agenda will help you to stop reacting so personally to their actions.

Which leads me on perfectly to the other function of the sacral chakra, **PASSION** for life and **GOALS**.

Passion and Goals

Having goals in life, being able to have a dream is vital and stems from this beautiful sacral chakra. But mustering up the passion is sometimes difficult when you allow yourself to focus on the negative. So, remember the same rule still applies:you get what you think of from the universe. So, when you have a goal set or a plan of something to achieve or work towards, focus on the end result with everything you've got. *FEEL* the *JOY* and excitement when you imagine and visualize living your dream. Make every part of your thinking match with what life will be like when you hit your goal. The passion is pure *JOY* of every step of the journey. It comes from happiness that we spoke about earlier. When

Brian's Guide to Manifesting an Awesome Life.

you are happy, you can feel passion at the idea of more happiness coming into your life.

If you give your energy to any potential problems, you will have more problems. It is true isn't it when you say that when something goes wrong it tends to happen in threes. Why is this? Because you have just put power into that statement and believed it with such passion that you are waiting for the next 2 things to go wrong. When you are engulfed in grief and anxiety and another bad thing happens, it is so easy to act as if you expected more bad times to come because, hey, that is your luck at the moment. You again have given the energy to things going wrong. So of course, you will not be surprised to see that it indeed went wrong. It is very easy to call it a run of bad luck. But there is no such thing. You created that through your thoughts and the universe is stood behind you pointing out that you asked for that with your thoughts and feelings.

So, lets focus on the goals. You can have anything you want and desire, but what do you actually want? You have learnt to cut the ties to people or situations that held your power, so now anyone else's opinion of whether you are worthy or have a chance of being able to be successful in achieving your goal in life doesn't come into it. This is just between you and the universe now.

So, with all negative thoughts gone, please write down what your main goal is in life.

Brian's Guide to Manifesting an Awesome Life.

No room for limitations here, so if your goal is to own your own home with enough bedrooms to fit your brood in plus a home cinema, then go ahead, write it down and **FEEL** the **JOY** of living in a house like that.

If you begin to question how the actual hell you are going to be able to afford such a house, then go back to square one because you have just told yourself with that negative thought that it's all down to you to earn the money to buy the house. You have instantly cut out the universe and its helpers and taken on the whole responsibility yourself. We do not need details here, you don't need to write down how we are going to achieve the goals, we just want the goals.

Maybe your goal is to have children, but right now you don't have a partner, and you have been told you have a medical problem that means you can't have children.

This is a biggy. Probably bigger than the biggest house you could wish for, because this one involves removing MASSIVE negative beliefs that you have in place. Or is it? Because isn't it just the same as we have spoken about already, where you give your power to another human being, namely the doctor who said you can't have children. Or to the ex-partner that left before you had the chance to have children?

So again, please write down your goal, without a single block in sight or thought.

Brian's Guide to Manifesting an Awesome Life.

But write your goals as if you already have them.

For example:

I want to have children = I have children

I want to own a house = I own a house

Get my drift? Now say it, read it out loud with pure ***PASSION*** and ***BELIEF.*** Then put it away and get on with your day. If you keep asking for the same thing, you are effectively double checking that we heard you and you must be feeling doubt as otherwise you would not be asking a second or third time. If you asked a friend to get you something from the other room, you wouldn't ask them again and again as they walked to fetch it for you, so don't do the same with us. Believe with every inch of your energy that we heard you because we did.

So, if it was having children you set as your goal, check how you respond when other people around you become pregnant. Do you become filled with jealousy or envy? Do you find yourself moaning under your breath that it is not fair because she or he already have far too many children? Do you find yourself feeling negative thoughts about how someone else raises their children?

Brian's Guide to Manifesting an Awesome Life.

Remember, it is all about the energy you **FEEL** with anything and everything.

If your goal is to have a successful business, you need to be excited every step of the way. This includes when you check out the competition and see how well they are doing. If feelings of jealousy and envy and plans to beat, undercut or sabotage creep into your mind, we have a problem being able to bring your success to you. Passion and excitement, when you see an example of another company doing the same idea successfully should fill you, encouraging you that your idea is indeed possible! Joy and utter elation that you have just been shown you are onto something that may be exactly as great as you want it to be!

Thoughts towards the competitor should be from a place of love and hoping that they continue with their success, remembering that everyone is entitled to achieving their goals and are not actually in competition with you! You and the competitor actually have a lot in common, you are both striving in the same way of work which means you have a lot of the same qualities and experiences. Rooting for each other to be successful is not only nice but transforms the energy flowing through you to a positive successful one!

If your goal is to have a bigger and better house, I understand it is hard to be happy with your current smaller one, but oh boy it is so important that you begin

Brian's Guide to Manifesting an Awesome Life.

to appreciate everything you do have. If you are constantly moaning about the one you live in now, how the hell can you be giving positive energy to manifesting your next one? If you are only focused on talking about the things you aren't happy about such as the small kitchen, not enough bedrooms, the leaking roof and so on, then you aren't giving the passion toward having a beautiful perfect new home.

So, change your ways dramatically and instantly. Start saying what you ***LOVE*** about your house or life right now. List the positives and ***FEEL PASSION*** for what you love. When you drive past the kind of house you visualize yourself living in, you should be filled with pure joy at the sight of it. Positive statements should roll of your tongue listing why you love the house you are looking at.

It is such a perfect location!

The driveway will fit my car perfectly!

The garden is gorgeous! I LOVE IT!

It looks simply perfect to me!

The feeling of butterflies in your lower tummy will kick in and you may even find yourself doing an air punch or have a huge grin just like you did when you got your dream bike as a kid at Christmas. Then you know

Brian's Guide to Manifesting an Awesome Life.

you are on the right path and aligned beautifully with the universe. ITS ON ITS WAY!

Go home and keep that feeling of excitement. You got this. Do not let anything take that feeling away from you. When you get back to your existing house don't feel deflated, instead see it as an incredible opportunity to visualize what the dream house you just saw from the outside, actually looks like on the inside! Start redesigning the house in your mind, look at your current kitchen and POSITIVELY improve it in your mind. Where would you move the cooker and where is the dishwasher that you haven't yet got, going to go? What kind of cupboard doors will you have and what sort of tiles?

What if your goal is to achieve something like becoming a top professional in a sport you love? To reach the top of your chosen field and win win win?

It gets daunting when you look ahead and see everything you have to achieve along the way in order to get there and its harder when it's just you alone and your success purely relies on your effort and physical success alone. Like a lone athlete, who doesn't have a team to be a part of, or a solo singer who doesn't have band members to share the stage nerves with.

Well, you are not alone. You are connected to the universe and the process of succeeding is exactly the same as for all the other examples such as having a house or family.

Brian's Guide to Manifesting an Awesome Life.

Write down exactly what you want as if you have already achieved it. And BELIEVE IT.

I want to be a successful…. = I AM a successful…...

This is already true if you think about it because you are already doing the sport or talent in your everyday life. You have already worked out what it is you want to become or do, which is more than a lot of young people. You have already found your **PASSION** and **JOY** in life therefore you are one step ahead to achieving your goal.

Again, every moment you have a negative thought or the road to success becomes daunting, pull yourself back to ***en-JOY-ing*** the sport. Go back to **FEELING** the *passion* for what you are training for. If the passion goes, ask yourself why this is so. Are you putting too much pressure on winning and forgetting the original feeling you so loved when playing the game? Is your insecurity and lack of self-belief making you focus on your competitor? Are you filled with negative thoughts such as envy and jealousy when you see someone else win? Or are you filled with excitement and genuine happiness to see them achieve their goals? Rooting for your opponents is vital.

Hmmm was that last sentence hard to swallow? Because surely, you have to put all your energy into being

Brian's Guide to Manifesting an Awesome Life.

better than your opponents in order to WIN. Nope. You have to put all your energy into being the best you can be and you are at your best when you are relaxed, happy and passionate about being on the path to achieve your GOALS.

So no more wasting energy on who you are up against or who you must beat. They do not have anything to do with you achieving your goal of winning. You do. Remember to open up to the universe and allow that divine free flowing energy to flow through your body, removing all negative, insecure doubts and remind yourself your soul/sole purpose in life is to experience the emotion you set as an intention in your root chakra. Only thinking of the pure pleasure, the sport gives you and why you originally began to play it.

It really is simple. Do not over complicate it. **FEEL** the love of the game, keep the **PASSION** for the game you so **LOVE**.

So, as you continue with your daily life, having set your goals, miracles can now begin. All the work you have done already begins to show results. The universe just needs you to focus on the positive feelings and thoughts, enjoying every step you take through life without a single negative thought and it will do the rest for you. Opportunities will present themselves to you out of nowhere. People who can help will be brought to your attention. New paths will appear in life and all you must

Brian's Guide to Manifesting an Awesome Life.

do is take them constantly saying YES and THANKYOU as you go.

Now that the universe can work with you, magic begins to happen. When something incredible happens that brings your goal one step closer to you, get as excited as you did when you won that money on the bingo or lottery that time. Get as excited as you did when you were the kid at Christmas receiving the present you had been waiting for all year that you didn't think you'd ever get. Be as stupidly thrilled as you possibly can and *FEEL* the GRATITUDE WITH EVERY OUNCE OF YOUR BODY.

ITS WORKING!!!!

Now don't blow it, by trying to take control of what's coming next. Do not try to preempt what that opportunity or person who has suddenly appeared in your life is going to lead to. Accept it for what it is, in the here and now. Focus on how it helps now at this stage in your path to success. This is because if you look forward too much you will be second guessing and creating or imagining possible problems or stumbling blocks and delay the process. For example, let us say an opportunity to connect with a coach in another country comes up. If the first thing you think of is how the logistics will work out, being able to afford the flight, take the time off and where the heck will you stay, you will wreck and stop the flow of incredible energy that is following your thoughts of successfully achieving your

Brian's Guide to Manifesting an Awesome Life.

goal. If, however, you just **TRUST** and say thank you like a grinning hyena you will see that even the money for the flights and the accommodation flow to you just as easily as the original opportunity. If you let it.

A classic example of this involves a lady that we all know too well in my life.

Her daughter had an amazing opportunity while studying to become a chef to go and do a month's work experience in the Hamptons NY. It wasn't financed, she would have to fund the entire trip herself, but this didn't faze her. The fact that she only just about had the rent and bills covered each month without a penny in savings did not put her off. She told her daughter that absolutely, yes, she would be going and immediately began arranging the details with the restaurant via email as to what dates they would arrive and what benefit her daughter would gain from working in a top restaurant that served celebrities on a daily basis.

She then carried on with her daily life and asked us to take the anxiety away and sort the details out. So, she let us in and ASKED us to help.

Her and her young son where due to go to Scotland for a lovely weekend away just the two of them and left the older girls at home alone in Cornwall. One of the dogs was on heat and the last instruction she screamed at the girls as she went out the door was to not forget to keep the dogs in separate rooms at all times.

Brian's Guide to Manifesting an Awesome Life.

She came back two days later to her girls nervously explaining that nothing happened between the dogs, but it nearly did, and they had booked the male dog into the vets for the chop the next day. Leila the daughter who was training to be a chef had even paid for it already, so she didn't have to worry.

You guessed it; the dog got pregnant. But this lady didn't get angry, she laughed. She laughed so hard as she knew what this was leading to. She even correctly guessed the number of puppies that were about to be born. 3, the same number as the bums on seats on the flights she needed to get to America. One for her daughter, one for her and one for her son as she was not leaving him behind for a month. She screamed with pure *JOY* as she realized how amazing this all was and that it was not really a problem, it was a solution that she hadn't and wouldn't ever have, thought of herself. She acknowledged how awesome the universe is around her and that her prayers had indeed been answered.

She *en-JOY-ed* the experience of watching puppies in the house instead of worrying and complaining about the mess, noise and lack of sleep. It was a fantastic experience for all the family to experience together. She sold them to friends who she would be able to keep in contact with and carry on watching the progress of these adorable little souls. And she slapped down the cash for the three flights and high fived her kids.

Brian's Guide to Manifesting an Awesome Life.

So, realising how easily and effortlessly the money for the flights came to her, she didn't even worry about the accommodation. She just carried on with her life and KNEW that that would be sorted too. They excitedly searched for apartments to be able to rent for a month with just the road name of the restaurant her daughter would be working in each day to make sure she would be able to walk safely to each shift.

Then about a month later, she suddenly had the thought that her tax return would be due while she was away in the Hamptons and she decided to be prepared for once and fill out the tax returns on time. Imagine the sound of laughter when she realised she was owed tax back, strangely the exact amount that she needed to pay for a month's accommodation. So, following the feeling of having to complete the boring tax return brought the unexpected answer to a problem she didn't give energy to.

So, something as huge as a month's trip for three people abroad for a single mum with no savings suddenly became a reality. Anything is possible for everyone!

The path that they followed with only trust and faith led to so much more. A year later, because of the experience of a top NY restaurant and the glowing reference from the owner, her daughter was offered a fantastic fulltime job in a Michelin star restaurant in London.

Brian's Guide to Manifesting an Awesome Life.

Be prepared to go with the flow of the universe as your goal is being manifested, because you cannot stay where you are if you have asked for change.

This is where a lot of you go wrong, suddenly setting limitations when you see the first change occurring. You put on the brakes and say no to being open to change. If you have set your goal as being able to buy a house of your own, then the way you work and earn money is going to have to change too. If you refuse to move the children out of their local school, then you need to stipulate and detail your goal to match.

I own a house = I own a house in this neighbourhood.

But then again, if you are open to the stupendous limitless possibilities the universe is capable of bringing you, you won't set limitations at all. You will be excited to go with the flow and **TRUST** that there is a much bigger picture that you are a glorious part of. You will **FEEL** in the core of your being that there are so so many amazing things that you are worthy of receiving and that they are on their way to you in incredible ways.

If you are setting limitations, you would be wise to take a moment and see what your FEAR is of change. What is it that you are afraid of losing and why? Is it a material possession that you don't want to give up? If so, why are you putting all your energy and intent into a

Brian's Guide to Manifesting an Awesome Life.

possession? If it is a person then you must work out why you are giving all your power and energy to that person. What are you afraid of? Remind yourself that the only person you are in control of is you and others are free to make their own choices and decisions. Maybe their goals are different and lead them to different paths in life. Make a list and break it down bit by bit. What is holding you back. What are you not prepared to give up to be able to achieve what your goal is? Then the most important bit to work out is why.

So, to kick start this incredible chakra there is a simple technique that you can put into practice daily. It is so simple you may even laugh.

Breathe like you used to when you were an uncomplicated child. Watch a baby breathe and you will see their stomach inflates with each breathe in and deflates with every breath out.

Try it and see how instantly you feel calmer. You will notice how it takes the pressure and anxiety off your chest because you're not just focusing on inhaling and exhaling with your lungs. As you put the focus on inflating and deflating your stomach instead, you will be using your entire lung capacity with ease, instead of tensely breathing and using the top half of your lungs only. So, by allowing the sacral chakra to flow and spin beautifully you are also having a positive effect on your chest and heart chakra without even knowing it.

Brian's Guide to Manifesting an Awesome Life.

See the body as a truly magical thing that you have been blessed with. It has all the answers and tools built into it that you need to function properly and healthily, both physically and mentally.

So, remember when we said to follow what brings you the word or intention that you set in your root chakra? Every single time you find yourself feeling fear, doubt or anxiety, every time you find yourself trying to control or see exactly how you will achieve your goal, every time you find yourself not being passionate about your life, you must go do something that brings you the *JOY* immediately. Eat the cheese, water the garden, do your hobby, sleep. Just do it. Stay in the here and now and in the *JOY*. While you're giving *your-SELF* the feeling of *JOY*, more joy can come to you, as you show the universe how happy you are to feel so god damn good.

Now you can see how much you have affected the sacral chakras ability by tensing up your body and focusing on the anxiety and stress that you have felt. You have literally tensed your stomach and crunched it up when you felt un-ease. This has unknowingly not only affected your physical body, but it has also played a part in preventing you from manifesting your goals with pure passion.

SO, BREATHE!

Try it when you feel anxiety and fear creeping in. Reconnect to the divine love of the universe from the top

Brian's Guide to Manifesting an Awesome Life.

of your head, watch that light flow through your body again and breathe the way your body was designed to , filling your stomach with air as you go. You will find the anxiety leaves your being very quickly, allowing you to focus on the positive again without any blocks.

To Do List

Breathe with your stomach, not your lungs

Focus on what brings you *JOY*

Laugh at every given opportunity

Go with the flow of the universe

Eat the cheese.

Brian's Guide to Manifesting an Awesome Life.

CHAPTER SIX:

Clearing the Way Forward

The universe that works with you and through you is not only affected by your negative thoughts but also by the things in your life that surround you on a daily basis. Not only is it important that your body is a clear channel, but the energy needs to be able to flow freely through your life too.

So, what do your surroundings say about how you really *feel?*

So now we need to assess the space you live and work in. If you are manifesting **LOVE** into your life, what memories of an experience of love are you holding onto and unwittingly using to block achieving your new goal? Do you still have photographs of your last relationship tucked away in a drawer or worse, your last wedding dress stored under the bed, even though you divorced years ago?

If you are manifesting financial stability and abundance, you need to look at how you treat money and bills right now. Is your house filled with bills stacked up in a pile in the corner, unopened and forgotten about? Are you carefree with money, leaving loose change everywhere and anywhere? Or do you have a pot where you save all change you have and limit the money you allow yourself to spend? What is the state of your purse or wallet? Is it filled with receipts and out of date

Brian's Guide to Manifesting an Awesome Life.

vouchers,coupons and store cards that you don't ever use? Or is it organized and clear of clutter, proudly saying this is where I can access all my money, and this is where new money comes to. Is the purse or wallet tatty and broken or is it clean, new and an item you love to see?

    Do you unwittingly tell yourself that you are not worthy of a certain item or price range? The lady we all know a little too well in my life, only realised whilst doing the online course for this book that she had a negative thought about an up-market supermarket. Her mother had always shopped in it when she was a child and she had associated it with being expensive, out of her range and only for rich people. She had shopped in every other supermarket chain invented as an adult herself, but never this one. She had even passed this thought onto her girls without knowing. They had spent their entire childhood being told that this chain was triple the price of everything because grandma shopped there. They all knew it was filled with lovely luxury items, but all believed they were overpriced because mum had said so. Until, one day only a few months ago, the overwhelming need for coffee to give her a caffeine fix, meant she had no choice but to enter that particular chain of shops. She had begun to learn the "I am worthy" line and kept reminding herself that she deserved a nice extra special upper class triple the price packet of coffee. But as she walked through the automatic doors, she came head on with the biggest shock of her life. There was a

Brian's Guide to Manifesting an Awesome Life.

huge display of boxes of chocolates, her children's favourite savoury snacks and mints, wrapped with beautiful bows on. Perfect for special occasions and gifts. ALL CHEAPER THAN HER REGULAR HIGH STREET SUPERMARKET!

Laughing out loud and grabbing one of each, she walked to the coffee aisle. There was a gorgeous gold packet of Arabic roast strength 5 ground coffee for HALF THE PRICE OF HER CHEAP UNBRANDED ONE SHE DRANK EACH WEEK!

Needless to say, now she happily shops in the supermarket that she believed she couldn't afford or wasn't posh enough to shop in, for her whole god damn life.

Look around the room you spend the most time in your home and tell me, is it organized, clear or messy and full of stuff that really belongs in another room or area of your house?

Is the beautiful rug that you once proudly and excitedly spent quite a lot of money on, now dirty, stained or covered in children's toys?

Is the sofa that you sit on in need of a clean, is it broken or worse, is it hidden under a pile of washing waiting to be cleaned or ironed? Are you using it for its real purpose or as a place to stack stuff that you do not really know what to do with?

Brian's Guide to Manifesting an Awesome Life.

When the kitchen cupboards are opened, can you see instantly everything that you have or are they unorganized?

Do you have kitchen drawers that get stuck when you try and open them as they are filled to the brim with stuff that doesn't really belong in them?

What is your front door like? Inviting for people and new ideas and opportunities to enter, or is it dirty, blocked and giving the message that you do not welcome new people.

Have you got windowsills or shelves crammed full of ornaments, photos and memorabilia of past times so much so that you cannot get the maximum enjoyment from each one? Is there dust dirt or stains around any of these ornaments, indicating that you have not admired them in a very longtime?

Thinking of your bedroom, your sacred private space in the entire house, does it look more like a storeroom than a bedroom or an office? Is the floor clear and does it look inviting when you walk in?

What is your wardrobe like? Is it full of clothes that don't fit you anymore just in case you may lose or put on the weight one day to be able to wear them again? Are you keeping hold of clothes because of the memory attached to the night you wore them last?

Can doors open fully into all rooms in the house or are there things stacked behind them?

Brian's Guide to Manifesting an Awesome Life.

Wherever you work from, maybe a home office or even a part of the kitchen where you keep important paperwork and bills, is it full of stuff that is no longer relevant? Do you have paperwork from bank accounts you no longer have or projects you worked on years ago?

Is the desk clear or does it have dust, rubbish and empty coffee cups on it?

Have you ever walked into a room, and felt depressed for no particular reason? That is the energy you are feeling and picking up on. The same way you feel depressed anxious and stuck, the energy around you can feel the same.

You know what I am going to tell you to do next don't you?

CLEAR IT

CHUCK IT

CLEAN IT!!

No excuses now please, the universe needs you to work with it not against it. Here to help you out a little is a simple feng shui plan or grid that you can use for the entire house floorplan as well as each individual room. If you do this thoroughly, you will see the positive effects instantly. You will feel better physically, emotionally and spiritually. You will have made way for the universe to bring you new things and begin to see the limitless

Brian's Guide to Manifesting an Awesome Life.

abundance that is waiting for you to grab. You will finally understand that you do not need to hold onto the past anymore, in fact you will see how doing that is holding you back.

Clearing out your wardrobe is a great place to start as its very personal to you, the old you and the new you. Be ruthless and maybe consider giving clothes away to a charity or thrift store. You want to be able to see what you have to wear, that fits you and that makes you happy to be up and dressed, not have a constant reminder that you no longer fit into half of the last decades fashion trends.

Throw away anything that doesn't serve its purpose anymore and items that are broken.

Pull furniture away from the walls just a few inches so that the energy can flow around all corners of the room.

Keep hallways and doorways clear again to let the energy flow freely.

The chart on the next page is a simple yet highly effective grid for you to be able to use to understand the energy in your home. It can be used for the entire house layout at once as well as each individual room that you have. Turn it round to match the bottom of the grid with the entrance to the room or house, so when you walk through the doorway, the top right-hand corner of the

Brian's Guide to Manifesting an Awesome Life.

room is always the **_LOVE_** corner. Divide the room into approximate equal squares and have fun sorting through your home.

One lady who plays a big part in my life, years ago hit a very rocky patch in her relationship with her husband. The arguments were off the scale and both began to wonder what the hell had happened suddenly. When they resorted to using this grid and discovered that they had accidentally placed their overflowing laundry bin in the love corner of the bedroom they both took the time to rearrange it together, laughing at how stupid they had been. Once the offending laundry bin had been moved out of the bedroom, the impact was felt by the both of them instantly. Their usual happy fun home life soon kicked in again.

The same lady only recently complained to herself that she did not have any friends in her life that could just pop round for coffee and a chat and she stressed how she wanted to change this. When she came to clear and reorganize her kitchen with this grid, she noticed in the bottom right corner of the kitchen there was a gorgeous shabby chic tray, set out with a tea pot, cups and saucers and a cute matching milk and sugar bowl, purely for display purposes as nobody ever came round to warrant using it. Looking closely, she found the milk jug contained odds and sods, like pencils, paperclips, a couple of screws and picture hooks and even one of her son's golf balls was in the teapot. When she went to move it, she found the entire tray was stuck down hard

Brian's Guide to Manifesting an Awesome Life.

thanks to water having seeped under the wooden tray many times over the last few months. She had to pull hard and finally shifted it, leaving half the bottom of the tray stuck to the kitchen work surface. Getting the gist of the message swiftly, she threw out the tray and cleaned all the cups and saucers and pots and rearranged them. Two days later, her friend from school days reconnected with her and messaged out of the blue. Turned out, they only lived 20 minutes away from each other! There was the friend she so wanted to be able to share a coffee and a natter with finally.

Brian's Guide to Manifesting an Awesome Life.

WEALTH AND PROPSERITY	REPUTATION AND FAME	LOVE
FAMILY AND COMMUNITY	HEALTH AND BALANCE	CREATIVITY AND CHILDREN
WISDOM	CAREER	FRIENDS AND TRAVEL

FRONT OF HOUSE / DOOR INTO ROOM

It can be quite daunting to know where to get started when you first begin clearing your space. I would suggest beginning with the area of your life that you

Brian's Guide to Manifesting an Awesome Life.

want to manifest better ways into first. So, if you are in a job that you absolutely detest, or running a business that needs to succeed much more quickly than it is right now, start with the bottom center of the room. If this is where the entrance to the room or house is, make sure you include the doorway itself, where new energy is flowing in from every time the door is opened.

Likewise, if you are wanting to manifest love into your life, begin with not only the top right corner but also the square area on the middle left, for family and community. If you are inviting a new relationship in, it will benefit and affect the entire family or may even create a family for you, who knows!

The front door is where new ideas and opportunities and even people come through. Ashtrays, dead plants, kids shoes and dog leads, bags of rubbish waiting to be collected all help to clog up the flow of energy. Keep it clear and clean. Every once in a while, scrub the doorstep with salt and hot water, especially when you're waiting for good news. If you're feeling really enthusiastic, you could always give the actual door itself a new coat of paint.

Interesting that the center of the room is your health do not you think? The one thing that is vital for you to continue being able to live life to the full. Keep all centers of rooms clear for the energy to flow freely, remove or at least tidy coffee tables plonked in the

Brian's Guide to Manifesting an Awesome Life.

middle of the lounge. If your bed is in the center of the bedroom, it's actually a great place for it to be, but check what is shoved under it or sort the drawers under it if you have any. Plus, make your bed each morning you get up. Keep it fresh and clean and tidy. Your sleep is paramount for a healthy physical body as it restores the energy and recharges your battery each night.

Warning: Using Feng shui in your house will become addictive. You will soon feel the difference and start searching for what is wrongly placed in a room when you enter it. This can't do any harm at all, instead it's actually a great sign that you are beginning to en-JOY and cherish your home and value your life. It shows you're taking pride in your surroundings and starting to have a sense of belonging. It also gives you a taste of how necessary and powerful the universe is around you.

I am sure you have heard of vision boards where some folk say they are a great way to entice things you desire into your life. I fully agree apart from one thing. It shouldn't just be filled with materialistic things you want to buy. If you get the board right, it should be filled with items and situations that bring you the word or emotion that you set as your intention in the root chakra. So, ***JOY***, ***LOVE*** or ***HAPPINESS***. Just focus on the emotion that you will bring into your life.

Cut out pictures from magazines, use photographs, print off the word such as JOY in big bold letters and place it in the center of the vision board. It

Brian's Guide to Manifesting an Awesome Life.

can still be a glorious car or house that you want to manifest, but you're not just wanting a lovely car, you're wanting to attract the emotion or feeling it will bring into your life. Utter, overwhelmingly awesome complete ***JOY. Feel*** it in the core of your being like when you were a child, watching a Lamborghini zoom past you in the street, remembering the feeling of excitement the roar of the engine gave you. When you feel that excitement, then choose which picture you are going to place on your board. Remove all limitations in your mind, such as the practicalities of having a Lamborghini on your driveway or taking you to your job at the coffee shop. Or the cost of running it. Or what other people would say about you having a car like that. All those negative thoughts stop the car in its tracks. Literally. If it's the emotion you've focused on, then the car you receive will give you the exact same feeling and you will be so damn excited to own it, you will love every second of driving it. It may well be a different make or model of car, but it will be perfect in every single way. So, no limitations please, as the universe remember has limitless amounts of abundance it can bring to you, if you let it.

      Maybe it is a holiday that you would like to put on your vision board. Take the time to scroll through different destinations and when you find the one that makes your stomach feel like it has butterflies in it, cut out the picture and place it on the board. Do not even

Brian's Guide to Manifesting an Awesome Life.

question how you will afford it, that's not your problem, that's ours. If it brings you JOY, put it on your board.

If it is a relationship or creating a family you want to manifest into your life, first remove all thoughts of previous relationships and also of a particular person. Remember you cannot control another human being and they have their own free will and paths to live in life. You must not fix your solutions or hopes and dreams to another human. Instead, put the word LOVE on your board, but take the time first to look at pictures, read stories or think of beautiful love stories that have a wonderful happy ending. **FEEL** the love, the ache in your heart as you think of an elderly couple who are still happy together, holding hands at the age of 82. How beautiful is that, unconditional love for each other after children and grandchildren too. Think back to when you have been blissfully in love and recall the positive physical feeling it gave you at the time. All relationships were good at the start, so do not focus on how the past relationship ended, just the feeling you alone had in your heart,when love and a relationship began.

If it is becoming successful at a chosen sport or winning a competition one day, the highlight of your future career and achieving your goal, then simply place a picture of your goal. A photograph of the competition you want to be a contestant in, a picture of the grounds or trophy you will win. Take the time to work out

Brian's Guide to Manifesting an Awesome Life.

logically how old you will be when the opportunity comes and write the year next to the trophy. But remember, it's all about the emotion you feel when you think of winning that trophy, so if you have a single iota of doubt and lack of self-belief, then keep looking at the photos, open up to the divine light, draw down that incredible unconditional love from the universe, fill your entire being with the energy, remove all fear and lack of self-worth, allow yourself to be your best friend, believing and supporting and rooting for you to achieve your dreams. Do you *feel* it yet? Do you feel the excitement of winning? Imagine who is there supporting you. Who else is your biggest fan? Who can you ***SEE*** that is cheering you on, having watched you through your entire life training for this day? Is it your mum, is it your gran, is it your husband or wife? Who is there celebrating with you? Can you feel what your reaction will be yet, when you get your hands on the trophy and hold it high above your head? Can you see the photographers taking your photograph for the front page of their magazine or paper? Can you HEAR the bustle and excitement around you as everybody cheers and celebrates with you? You got it my friend, now write that feeling down of winning next to the picture of that amazing trophy. It's yours.

    As you achieve things in your life, you can change the pictures on the board. As you go through life with the mind set of going with the flow, your goals and desires can change. This is a good thing. As your job

Brian's Guide to Manifesting an Awesome Life.

changes, as your finances improve, you may find your choices do too. Or when you achieve the new job, the new relationship, your focus can shift onto another goal. Keep the board placed in an area of your house or room where you see it on a regular basis. It becomes a part of your life so should not be put away in a drawer or cupboard.

To Do List

Clean your personal space!

Make a vision board of things that bring you JOY

Brian's Guide to Manifesting an Awesome Life.

CHAPTER SEVEN:

The Solar Plexus Chakra

The Solar Plexus is, as are all the others, a crucial chakra to keep healthy. Think of it like a built-in communication center with the universe. If you can't yet see or hear your guides, this is the one you use to be able to feel *FEEL* their guidance. This chakra is where your **personal power**, **confidence**, **gut feeling**, and **knowing** come from. When it spins healthily you can confidently walk through life following the feeling inside that lets you unequivocally know that you are going in the right direction and doing the right thing. It is like a built-in buzzer that lets you know instantly if you go off course, or bump into the barriers, and tells you to readjust your path. When spinning healthily you don't give a hoot what other people's opinions are of you ,as you just *KNOW* that this is the right decision for you. You *FEEL* the guidance and approval from the universe, and you walk confidently through life.

When it isn't healthy and you don't listen or work with it, you will feel anxiety, the stomach-churning sensation of living on your nerves all the time. Physical ailments involving the gut, acid reflux, ulcers, pancreas problems, blood sugar issues and an entire range of health issues with the intestines and even kidneys can begin and cause you even more discomfort on top of the anxiety.

Brian's Guide to Manifesting an Awesome Life.

It spins a beautiful bright canary yellow colour and is situated in the core of your being by the stomach, just under the ribs or sternum bone. Before you rush to the doctors and take the prescription for indigestion or anti-depressants for the anxiety and panic attacks, let's do some work together on this chakra first.

Personal Power

Your personal power is unstoppable once you have reclaimed it from the people or past situations you gave it to through fear or self-doubt. It is the force inside of you that gives you the determination and strength to go through with an idea or action. It is the feeling that you can do anything and that you have the right and are worthy of something.

Once you have removed all the negative feelings and all the fear that you have believed up until now, you are left with hope. Hope feels exciting as it runs through your body giving you the belief that something is indeed possible. It needs effort to add to the mix then we have an action which leads to a result. Taking action is recognising your power is all you need to get to somewhere, achieve something or become something.

Fear is an easy option or excuse, but it hasn't led to success anytime in your life. The ability to overcome that fear and turn it into an adrenalin is within you as a natural human ability and it creates miracles when you

Brian's Guide to Manifesting an Awesome Life.

utilize this. It lets you overcome hurdles along the path in life. It fills you with determination and is the life force within you itself. It shows you CAN do ANYTHING if you believe in *your-SELF*.

Personal responsibility comes in here again, as you see that you are responsible for your choices and actions in life. Nobody owes you anything. If another person does something for you, it is their choice to do so and they can also choose to stop. Wasting energy on arguing or trying to convince someone else to continue to finance you or love you is just that: wasted energy. Imagine what you could achieve if you put all that effort into your dreams and goals and life itself, instead of trying to justify why someone else should do it for you. Fear is what drives humans to become nasty or angry and manipulative. It is a negative emotion that comes from not seeing your own power, only focusing on the fact that another human has just cut theirs.

So we have learnt in the first few chapters about how to cut the power that other people and past situations have over us, now you have to face up to the fact that you have been relying on some peoples power instead of your own.

A perfect example of this is when your parents tell you it's time you contributed to the cost of living and pay rent. Life was comfortable for a while there; you know the time after you officially became an adult and finished being a dependent child. You got a job, you

Brian's Guide to Manifesting an Awesome Life.

earned your own money and were enjoying spending it on beer, smokes and a social life. Your parents began to realise that the financial struggle they had experienced *by choice* could get better now you are living in their house and bringing in money too. So, they ask for you to contribute, treating you like a fellow adult instead of a child. Maybe you did not like it. Do not beat yourself up as you remember the childlike sulks or thoughts that crossed your mind, they were all a natural part of maturing. The important thing to see is that your parents don't owe you anything whatsoever after you start to earn your own money and continue to live under their roof. Your personal power will help you respect them and your COMPASSION that we learnt about in the sacral chakra begins to kick in, helping you see things from their point of view.

What about when a relationship ends, and you weren't expecting it or wanting it to end. When someone breaks up with you or leaves your life and suddenly you find out you relied on them in so many ways that you did not realise. Finances are now your sole responsibility, decision making, social life, friends, you name it, every part of your life must change now you are alone. The whole time you are having to learn to stand alone in life and start all over again, you are having to battle with feelings of grief, rejection and fear. As painful as it is, wasting energy on trying to get that other human being to change their mind and justify why, won't lead to happiness. Even if that person does come back into your

Brian's Guide to Manifesting an Awesome Life.

life, you must see that you are an independent person, a unique soul who has the power to achieve your own goals and dreams in life.

    The same applies when you are made redundant or sacked at work and don't have a plan B. So many people hold on to the shock and anger and will put all their energy to fighting to receive compensation, justification or an apology. What's the point? How would life really be if you went back to the job, knowing you were there because a lawsuit said you could be? It would change the atmosphere and relationships between your colleagues, right? Or the feeling of satisfaction of winning compensation to prove you were wrongly treated won't last long and the money will run out. All the time, you are resisting help that the universe is bringing to you. Remember, go with the flow of energy. The right thing to do is to accept the change, channel that divine amazing light from above you and use your personal power to move forward in life, not back, to the next chapter awaiting you. Maybe just maybe, there is a better job or relationship for you to experience as you grow in ***your-SELF*** and the universe has brought these necessary changes while leading you to your goal that you are manifesting!

    This is the time to watch how you speak about yourself. If you catch yourself saying you cannot do something, stick the word "yet" on

Brian's Guide to Manifesting an Awesome Life.

the end of it. A tiny word but a huge difference to your statement about yourself. It says you are aware you cannot do something yet, but you haven't given up and you have many more chances to try. It says you are open to trying as many times as is necessary until you succeed. It changes your intention from a negative to a positive, stating that you are willing to keep on trying. Remember your new best friend – you, needs you to be positive and encouraging. Believe in them and they will flourish like anyone else you'd offer your support to.

Confidence

Once you have acknowledged your personal power, confidence will come naturally. This is not arrogance; it is a sign that you have found your inner strength after trying something without having to ask or rely on another person. It comes after using your personal power. It comes naturally when you have succeeded at something you never believed that you would be able to do. It *FEELS* like a sense of exciting satisfaction. It comes when you have removed all negative thoughts that you held onto for so long that you were not worthy or not good enough. It comes after you begin to treat yourself as your best friend, looking out for their every need and feeding your soul with LOVE. It comes when you know your worth.

If you need to boost your confidence a little, use phrases such as

Brian's Guide to Manifesting an Awesome Life.

I am worth it

I am capable

Repeat them a few times while breathing in and out deeply, filling your stomach with each breath as you do. Draw on the divine unconditional love that flows from the universe, breathing it in through every ounce of your body. Feel the support and love that surrounds you. You are never alone, and the world is not against you. Quite the opposite in fact, the universe is willing you to succeed and sees your worth every step of the way.

Gut Feeling

The gut feeling is the incredible way your physical body reacts or responds to the universe guiding you. It is proof that you are channeling at every second you breathe without even knowing it. Think of it as a built in buzzer that sounds off every time you touch the sidelines of the straight path you are on and the borders on each side are electric that buzz to keep you on the straight and narrow. Your stomach churns when you intuitively **FEEL** that something is not quite right.

What you do wrong, is feed that feeling with anxiety and doubt and end up making the feeling even

Brian's Guide to Manifesting an Awesome Life.

stronger. Remember that focusing on the negative in life only brings more and then searching for what could go wrong at that moment, stops you from being open to the beautiful divine guidance coming down from the universe as you try and CONTROL the problem. The universe was working with you perfectly, until you shut down and attempted to sort the issue all by yourself.

So, when you stomach churns, re connect with the free-flowing energy from above. Listen, see and feel the guidance that you were tapped into without knowing. If you were in the process of grabbing your car keys and heading out the door when your gut started churning, delay it for a moment, get a drink, busy yourself, go for a pee… Then when the feeling has passed, go back to what you were doing.

Remember that there is a bigger picture that you are a huge important part of. As a human, using your physical eyes and ears, you can only be aware of so much that is happening in your life. Connecting with the universe, you can "*see*" and "*feel*" what's ahead. Maybe, just maybe there was an accident waiting to happen five minutes into the future and a car was already careering round the corner into your road where you would have pulled out of your driveway. Maybe, just maybe, the stomach churning was to delay you by 30 seconds to prevent the accident from happening. Or maybe, it was an urgent call that was coming 2 minutes after you were leaving the house that you wouldn't want to miss.

Brian's Guide to Manifesting an Awesome Life.

What if the stomach churns when you can't stop what you're doing, like when you are in a competition and wanting to do your very best to win. What happens when nerves take over and your stomach churns? Well firstly, you have shut down, giving in to the overwhelming feeling of churning and sickness in the pit of your stomach. It may extend to the entire body, and make you feel sweaty, shaky and sick. Your initial reaction of taking control and thinking that you alone must get the next shot right ,or you'll screw up the entire chance of winning, doesn't help the situation at all. If you recognize that the stomach churn was there to give you a heads up or warning that if you continued the way you were, you might not be happy with the result, and you may want to channel the divine guidance from above to **HEAR** and **FEEL** the advice being given to you, you will be working in-tune with the universe and the stomach churning will stop as soon as you acknowledge it. Remember, let go of the control button, you are not alone in anything you do, the universe and its helpers are working with you beautifully every step of the way. They want you to win, they want you to achieve that utterly delicious emotion that you set as your intention in the root chakra – your soul/sole purpose in life – ***JOY! ELATION! HAPPINESS! LOVE OF LIFE!***

This is where you must have TRUST and FAITH and it will build up very quickly if you acknowledge

Brian's Guide to Manifesting an Awesome Life.

every time something amazing has happened that you could never have preempted by yourself.

Take a moment right now to acknowledge how in the past your gut feeling has been spot on in the most unexplainable way. Try and write down the times in your life where you can see that following your gut feeling has been right even when it didn't make any sense.

What about the times when you for no reason whatsoever other than your stomach churning before heading out, you decided to take an alternative route for a change, only to find out when you returned home that there had been a major accident on your regular route?

So, life becomes easier in so many simple regular daily situations when you are connected to the universe and listen to your amazing physical body. As you look after this chakra, it will get easier to recognize the way it is working with you and not against you.

How many times have you kicked yourself for not following your gut feeling about a person in your life? That stomach churning feeling when you first meet them and you instinctively know they're not good for you, but you dismissed it and it ended in disaster. Weeks, months or maybe years later, you say to yourself I damn well knew the first time I met them something was off, and you wish you'd listened. So, from this day forward, save yourself the heartache and be strong enough to listen to the gut. Your solar plexus chakra was trying to save you the trouble of the unnecessary lesson!

Brian's Guide to Manifesting an Awesome Life.

Knowing

So, this function of the chakra comes naturally after you've mastered the gut feeling function. You end up confidently walking around life just knowing and trusting that something is going to happen or that what you are doing is right. Yet you have the knowing that you don't need to know all the details, so you don't question or justify everything. You just KNOW! It comes from a place of trust and recognising that you are actually a part of the universe, you are connected to it and you are working in union with the divine magical awesome fluffy stuff and it feels AWESOME!!

The lady that we all know too well in my life even moved to the other end of the country for a coach for her sons golf without ever meeting him and without even having a place to live, or a school for her son to go to. The knowing that it was the right place, the right coach, the right time, when it meant leaving all her adult girls behind and connections and friends. She trusted that she was being guided and she did not question any of it. She followed the strong sense that it was right.

The school she chose for him, again following her gut feeling, was actually in a different county and involved a substantial drive each day but it didn't deter her. Turns out that in his class were 3 new friends for him that were also members of the same golfing academy, making his transition a happy and smooth one.

Brian's Guide to Manifesting an Awesome Life.

Within 8 months, all the girls were living close to her, having followed and she found all her old school friends were in the new area too. So, because she did the right thing for her son, she benefited greatly herself too.

To kick start this chakra there is a simple exercise I would like you to try.

Each time you feel the gut churn and you begin to engulf yourself with all the fear and negative thoughts, trying to work out what is wrong, I want you to imagine yourself taking the knot in the form of a huge ball out of your stomach and throwing it up to the sky. Ask for the universe to take that knot away and *SEE* it floating away and shattering into a thousand pieces. If you are actually worrying about a particular situation or problem and your stomach won't stop churning, ask them to take that problem away from you and again, see it shatter as it flies up to the sky away from you. Now put all your energy and focus on trusting, knowing that because you ASKED them for help, you have RECEIVED it.

Reopen the top of your head and allow the universe to flow through your entire body, flushing out all the negative blocks and fears that you are holding onto. Feel the love of the universe helping you and taking your problems away. Then go focus on something that brings you *JOY* – eat your favourite cheese, do

Brian's Guide to Manifesting an Awesome Life.

some arts and crafts or go for a walk. Anything, that doesn't involve the problem you were focusing on and everything that brings you a moment of feeling pure incredible *JOY*.

To Do List

Ask the universe for help with any and every problem and throw the knot of worry up to the sky.

Brian's Guide to Manifesting an Awesome Life.

CHAPTER EIGHT:
The Heart Chakra

The heart chakra when spinning healthily can be seen as two colours, pink and green. It affects not just the beating heart inside your body that is responsible for pumping the blood to all your vital organs, but it also affects the health of your lungs.

The easy and simple way to assess if your heart chakra is functioning healthily is to take a little look at how healthy your heart and lungs are. COPD, and asthma sufferers, read on. This one is for you.

The heart is the one organ that if it stops working, you're on the next plane out. It is an incredible organ that keeps beating even when you feel like it has been shattered into a thousand pieces. The heart chakra is the house of love and it is the center of your human body for a reason. The emotion LOVE is at the core of your existence. You ARE love, you are made from love and the stuff you are drawing down from the universe is pure unconditional LOVE. It is the making of you, it is what you all crave and search for this lifetime, it is what makes everything **FEEL** so good and the lack of it can literally break your heart.

The problem is you associate love with another human being. The love you feel for a child, a partner, a

Brian's Guide to Manifesting an Awesome Life.

parent. The love you feel for an animal in your life. You deprive yourself daily of all the love that is available to you in the universe and your world.

Love is all around. Love is the feeling you get when you are filled with ***JOY***. Love is the feeling you get when you witness love between two other people holding hands or stealing a kiss. You instantly focus on the fact that it isn't you who is enjoying the feeling of love at that moment in time and it reminds you of how much you are missing out on, but actually the universe has just shown you how good love feels and is waiting for your reaction to let it know if you are open to receiving it or not. Remember the universe responds to your emotions, so if you react at the sight of two people in love with jealousy, judgement or fear, you are effectively telling the universe you don't want any of that thanks, you're alright on your own experiencing the negative aspects of love, such as loneliness, rejection and loss.

When you accept love into your life UNCONDITIONALLY without enforcing rules and regulations upon yourself or the universe, you will laugh freely, smile until your face aches, be pain free, anxiety free and you will be able to ***SEE*** all the ways LOVE is beaming through you, around you and to you.

There are so many different parts of the emotion Love that you experience in a lifetime. The positive ones are easy, the painful ones are more difficult for you to let

Brian's Guide to Manifesting an Awesome Life.

go of. They have over time created deep rooted fears and insecurities within you that you now use as a wall to stop love entering your heart in case it hurts again. They have created beliefs in you that you deserve to suffer. Each time you have been hurt in love, you try and protect yourself the next time, stopping the love from flowing through you to heal.

    Ladies and gentlemen, love is the only thing that can heal a broken heart.

    So, grieving for the loss of a loved one is hard because the pain of losing love is so strong that you stop yourself from receiving it again. Doubled with the fact that you do not trust your judgment, you somehow blame yourself, searching for ways you could have or should have prevented such a tragedy from happening. You shut out the universe and the divine LOVE and you put all the responsibility on your own shoulders. This weighs you down and brings the negative feeling of guilt into your grief to make it harder for you to heal. You may even begin to believe the negative comments from other humans who, try as they might, haven't got a single clue as to how you are feeling, but voice their opinion. So, you give your power to another person, while searching for help and answers. You believe in other people's judgment more so than your own. When people judge your way of grieving and hurting, when they judge your way of trying to continue living, you end

Brian's Guide to Manifesting an Awesome Life.

up self-loathing and feeling unworthy of love ever again. You begin to believe what others say and join them in detesting yourself. Their words and actions reinforce how you already justify punishing yourself. Which, my friend, makes it so hard for the universe and its helpers to bring the much-needed medicine to fix your broken heart.

      What is that medicine? It is called LOVE.

      The lack of self-worth many of you feel is the biggest block you hold onto and stops love from being able to come into your life. I do not just mean the love of another person; I mean the love from the universe and the love for your-self.

      To heal this, we need to find the trigger point that started the feeling of unworthiness.

      The way you speak of yourself and the way you see yourself is crucial in being able to lead an awesome fulfilling life. It has nothing to do with any other human being in the world. It is all about you and your relationship with the universe. We have covered earlier on in this book about becoming your best friend, and rectifying all the damaging ways you speak to yourself and treat yourself as a second rate human being, but now we need to deal head on with what started that utter hate and contempt for your-self.

Brian's Guide to Manifesting an Awesome Life.

Think about your earliest memory of feeling a negative side to the emotion love. When did you first majorly feel and understand jealousy, envy, hurt, loss or rejection?

What happened after that feeling first hit and what negative thought about yourself did you take on, either first impressed upon you by another humans words and actions, or by yourself repeating them and holding onto them?

Did someone leave you without any explanation, did someone physically hurt you. Both these situations are the choice and responsibility of another human being, yet you are holding onto it as if it was your choice or fault. Your life since that day has been a process of reinforcing the pain and the action of believing that you deserved it, because it happened.

Let me be the one to tell you. IT WAS NOT YOUR FAULT. No excuses, no justifying anymore. It hasn't led you to happiness and not served you any purpose, so today is the day it stops.

Let go of the responsibility and hurt and throw it up to the universe to take it away. Give that thought and pain to us and you will feel lighter. Let the universe in!

Brian's Guide to Manifesting an Awesome Life.

What if you did something, maybe you were the one to leave or hurt someone. You must see that all the hate toward yourself hasn't changed the initial situation. It has not changed anything about the facts, it has only affected your life since. Your fear that your anger will rise to the surface in the next relationship has led you to believe that you are not to be around anyone as you may explode with rage and hurt someone again. You are constantly living in fear that someone else will see that side of you. So, your answer has been to punish yourself for years and years for the one thing you did and tell yourself that you are not worthy of love.

If this is you, then please LET IT GO. Accept responsibility and forgive yourself, seeing that you can move forward and ARE WORTHY of love just like anyone else.

See yourself as the little child you once were and imagine telling that child to their face that they will make one mistake in their life and for that they will suffer for the rest of their life. You would not let that child hold onto the guilt and pain and self-loathing so why do you do this to your-self?

FORGIVENESS is next. On the left hand side of a piece of paper, write down everything you hate yourself for, all the choices you made that you deeply regret and the ones that you die a little inside when you remember your actions or words. Now write down on the right hand side

Brian's Guide to Manifesting an Awesome Life.

of the paper, all the people or situations in your life that have brought you pain and hurt that you can't change from the past but whose words you've believed about yourself.

Take a moment to say sorry to anyone on that list that may have been affected in a hurtful way while you were learning to grow as a soul. Then apologise to your-SELF for all the unnecessary judging and hate you have directed towards yourself whilst on the journey through life.

Now rip it up with all the strength you have. Rip it into the tiniest of pieces and throw the damn thing up in the air. See all the little pieces float around you and onto the floor. That's it. Gone. Today is the first day of the rest of your life.

So being able to love your-self first is the key to having a healthy heart chakra. You all know through experience that focusing on loving others is a lot easier but allowing unconditional love to come to you because you know your worth, is essential. So, once you have loved yourself, you will stop accepting being second best to another person in life. You will be able to experience a happy and healthy relationship in love with another person, where you see your value as well as theirs.

So, take a moment now to give yourself a hug. You absolutely deserve a show of love, and you do not even need another person to give it to you. I want you to feel the love the universe has for you. Open up the top of

Brian's Guide to Manifesting an Awesome Life.

your head and let the divine love flow through your body all the way down your spine until it reaches your feet. Let it fill every part of your physical being. As you begin to feel the warmth of the energy in your body, place your hand on your heart. Take a deep breath in and as you breathe out push the golden light out of the palm of your hand and into your heart. Feel the surge of heat fill your heart and repeat for a few minutes until you begin to feel yourself receiving the love. Repeat the following phrase to yourself:

I AM WORTHY, I AM ENOUGH.

So, what is the magic answer to being able to feel love again? Gratitude.

GRATITUDE

Gratitude is the way to bring love back into your heart, soul and life. One step at a time, feeling and giving thanks for every small positive thing in your daily life.

Now there are lots of people that are aware that gratitude can bring utterly awesome miracles into their life after reading several books that tell you to list off what you are grateful for, explaining that it will soon double or triple the amount of things you will possess or receive. They are correct, but the simple key that is difficult and often misunderstood, is that you must

Brian's Guide to Manifesting an Awesome Life.

FEEL the gratitude. That has to come from you and can't be told or forced. You cannot just reel off a list of things you are happy about, you simply have to ***FEEL*** the emotion they bring you.

Remembering what we have been banging on about through this entire book is absolutely crucial now- the universe responds to the *feeling* you have with every ounce of your body as you ask the universe or give thanks for anything!

This will be pretty damn hard when you are feeling pain, loss, anxiety and depression through a broken heart. Nobody speaks of the physical pain that comes with raw grief, the crushing pressure that feels like you have an elephant sitting on your chest. The overwhelming feeling that you can't catch your breath and no matter how you sit or stand or rock back and forth, it just won't go away.

But you start at the beginning. You begin the day by acknowledging that you are your best friend and protector and you make sure that best friend is cared for. Just like if you were caring for a grieving friend or relative, you would bring them a cup of tea and a few biscuits to be able to do whatever you can to help in the smallest of ways, not focusing on the bigger problem that you cannot control. You ask that friend how they are feeling and what you can possibly do to help lighten their burden and brighten their day. You would assure

Brian's Guide to Manifesting an Awesome Life.

them you are not going anywhere, and you have all the time in the world to show them they are loved.

You would help them by praising them and getting them to acknowledge the smallest of good things throughout the day, trying to get them to see that there are some small positive things left in their world.

Now do this for yourself.

Give thanks for having a tea bag in the house to make the tea. Notice it is a damn fine cuppa at that moment. Smile at the realization it feels good wrapping your hands around the mug. Feel lucky for the fact there was milk left to colour it just the way you like. Give thanks for the fact the sun is shining when you look out of the window and acknowledge that this means you can sit outside at the very least or venture out to change the scenery. When you do venture out for a while, notice that it's a good job you put petrol in the car the day before as it made the day easier now.

Being RIDICULOUSLY POSITIVE about every little good thing that happens in your day is the way you can begin to *FEEL* positive and become genuinely grateful for everything you have. And being grateful for everything you have is the way to bring more of that *FEELING* into your life.

So being grateful for having filled up the tank of petrol the night before, without realizing you would need it badly the next day, isn't about the petrol itself, its

Brian's Guide to Manifesting an Awesome Life.

telling the universe you absolutely damn well LOVE the fact that you were one step ahead, worry free and have everything you need before you even need it ! It is helping you see that the universe is already there helping you and supporting you and bringing everything you need when you don't even realise it. You will be a little more open to receiving at that moment in time and a crack in the darkness in your heart will appear to be able to let more LOVE in.

Being able to *FEEL* the excitement of something good, is the way to bringing more good things to you very quickly. The moment you *FEEL* the utter *JOY* and *ELATION* of something coming into your life in the most magical way is the key to attracting more.

The woman in my life who we all know a little too well, took her inspiration from her son and her dogs while trying to learn how to have gratitude in her daily mundane life.

Every morning she would bundle three dogs and her son into the car and do the same routine of driving him to school and walking the dogs in the woods on the way back.

Her son would not be overly ecstatic about the fact he had to go to school and would have a mood on especially if the day ahead involved a lesson he particularly detested, but he would innocently change his attitude the moment he saw a sports car he could drool over, drive past.

Brian's Guide to Manifesting an Awesome Life.

He would scream for her to slow down so he could take a closer look. He would sit on the edge of the seat and glue his face to the window so he could see every single detail of the magnificent piece of machinery gliding past him. He would point in awe and declare that he would want one of those one day himself. He would then proceed to reel off all the facts he knew of how that beautiful car worked and how fast it was capable of going with pure passion.

She noticed that he was just simply grateful for the opportunity to see a car like that close up. It brought him utter ***JOY***. He declared what he absolutely loved without putting restrictions on it. He did not worry about how he would earn the money to have one himself one day, he just knew he would love to as it felt so good. He didn't sulk because it wasn't his car, he just enjoyed being able to appreciate it, see it and *feel* the ***JOY*** the creation of such a gorgeous car brought him.

She would drop her son off and turn the car round to go to the next stop which was always a walk in the woods about twenty minutes' drive away on the way back home. The dogs up until this point had been silent and well behaved in the back of the car, but the moment her son left the car and the engine started again, all three of the hounds would begin shouting, barking, jumping up and down with excitement and anticipation at where they were going. It was their turn and they damn well knew it. Their excitement could not be contained as she got closer and the barking turned into impatient whining.

Brian's Guide to Manifesting an Awesome Life.

The pull up to the woods entrance was always chaotic as they started to try and leap out of the car unable to cope with the sheer elation. She would scream and shout at them to be quiet and to calm down, but nothing worked. This one day she began to laugh and realised it was the same as her son experiencing pure joy at the sight of the sports car. She decided to join in with the screaming and barking and belly laughed so hard that she nearly peed herself. It felt good to be happy and it felt awesome at the thought of being able to walk in the woods with nothing else to worry about other than to enjoy the experience. It felt so great to be able to make the dogs happy like this and she realized that it wasn't a chore but a pleasure. She herself had joy from being able to switch off and just BE.

From that day on she made it a priority to walk further in the woods with the dogs. She scheduled it into her busy day and allowed her-SELF to benefit. She walked and walked, realizing she felt better within herself and happier. She breathed in the golden light and breathed with her belly naturally. She wiggled her root chakra and let her hips lead the way as she followed the dogs. She realized that she was able to walk better than she had ever done before in years as her diagnosis of COPD and all the meds she took each day, had dictated the amount of energy she had allowed herself to use.

Brian's Guide to Manifesting an Awesome Life.

Now, she allocates time for not one walk but two every day in her diary, including her-self in the list of priorities. She has after 6 months of doing this, increased her lung capacity, something that the medical profession told her was impossible and that she could only hope to maintain it and prevent it from getting worse. She has been able to stop using one of her inhalers permanently and no longer needs the pain killers. She has walked herself to health. In six months.

She remembered there had been a time not so long ago where she couldn't even walk up the stairs in her house without sitting down at the top. She recalled the conversation where the doctor had warned her if she didn't try and walk a little each day, she would be at the stage where she would need oxygen at the hospital. She remembered the time in the last house where she succumbed to the suffering and rearranged the house so her bedroom was downstairs, preventing her from having to even attempt the stairs, making it easier for her illness to take over.

As she walked through the woods, chasing the dogs she laughed out loud at the time when she tried to force herself to walk along the road she lived, only reaching the nearest lamppost before she had to turn back for her inhalers. She wished her doctor could see her now.

Brian's Guide to Manifesting an Awesome Life.

So allowing time for your new best friend and introducing pleasures and gifts for yourself the same way you do for everyone else you love, you will find your physical body responds pretty quickly to the love and attention you shower it with.

The ability to **FEEL** the love by being grateful for every little thing that brings you the feeling of joy, will allow more to flow to you. You will begin to see huge miracles come to your door, because you have stopped seeing yourself as unworthy.

So, having gratitude for what you have right now in your life, without worrying about the future or trying to work out what comes next, means you are fully living in the here and now. You are being present and aware of all the good things that you are surrounded by and how good life can actually be NOW.

Learning to see your worth and accepting love in, even if it's from you and not another human at first, helps to heal the pain you hold inside.

So, when you realise that your self-loathing and feelings of being unworthy are the reason that your finances, love life, wealth, health and luck are all suffering, it becomes so easy. Taking the time to process why you feel about yourself the way you do and why you have been so hard on yourself, is essential to change your thoughts. Then you can allow the love in and watch the magic begin in all areas of your life.

Brian's Guide to Manifesting an Awesome Life.

Practicing gratitude everyday will make you see how fast the universe works if you let it. It will also enable you to skip your way through the hard times in life, until you see that there is no such thing as bad luck, but there are miracles and positive outcomes in every single situation you could possibly find yourself in. It will help you see how utterly blessed you are when you let love in.

TO DO LIST

Hug yourself daily

Practice FEELING grateful for every tiny thing that brings you joy.

Stay in the here and now, every time you find yourself worrying about something that hasn't actually happened yet.

Brian's Guide to Manifesting an Awesome Life.

CHAPTER NINE:

Money

A lot of people have opinions that money, abundance and being a spiritual or 'good' person do not mix.

This is the same as every problem and block we have already covered so far in this book, but I want to talk it over with you. The block here to having the financial lifestyle you desire, is guilt. And you have put that block there.

Guilt of not wanting to be judged by others less fortunate because you don't want to show off.

Guilt of being financially flush when being spiritual as other people think you should be helping others for free.

Guilt of keeping money when there are less fortunate people in the world who need it more.

Guilt of having more money than you need.

I could continue, but you get my drift, right?

If you are in business and working your butt off at a craft that you have trained for years in at great expense, or have huge overheads running a business premises but you don't like to be greedy and charge

Brian's Guide to Manifesting an Awesome Life.

accordingly, or higher than the competitors as people may judge you, then you need to remind yourself of your worth. You happily paid to train with money and I bet you dreamed of a financially better way of living while you were investing in your career. You worked damn hard to get where you are now and you give your undivided attention, time and focus to each and every client or customer. You need paying for that.

It's coming back to lack of self-worth here isn't it folks? It's also showing the power that you have given to another person or situation in the past that you still need to cut off from. Did someone say once upon a time that what you do for a living is wrong, too pricey or a waste of time? Cut the ties man!

Do you genuinely believe in yourself and see that you are worthy of having an awesome and abundant life because you work so hard for it? But did someone say that you weren't really that good? Cut the ties now! That person has long gone, why are you still giving them your power and allowing them to affect your quality of life?

Your relationship with money began an awfully long time ago when you were a child. Can you try and think back for me the first time you realized money was an important part of the world?

The lady in my life who we all know a little too well, decided she would like to be broke forever when she was 11 years old. It was Christmas eve and her parents took her to a cheese and wine type posh party at

Brian's Guide to Manifesting an Awesome Life.

one of their friends' houses. All the children sat together eating crisps while the adults stood around the room chatting with the wine flowing. Her father called her over to where he was stood with a group of smartly dressed men, by the fireplace. He told her to say hello and introduce herself to each one in the group and so she did. "Hello, my name is Rhiannon" she said confidently, knowing her father was by her side.

All the men smiled politely and nodded, but one man dressed in a striped shirt with a strange coloured tie leant forward and said:

"What sort of a name is that! Don't your parents like you very much?" and began to laugh loudly, encouraging all the other men to laugh too.

Later, on the drive home, her father asked her what she thought of those men and she said that she did not like them at all because they were rude to her and laughed at her name.

Her father simply said, "Hmmm. You have just met your first millionaire."

From that moment on, she associated being a horrible person with being a millionaire and that ladies and gentlemen, is how easy it is to set an INTENTION.

So, what was your experience with money as a child because it is the reason you either love it or hate it. We need to undo that initial belief about yourself and

Brian's Guide to Manifesting an Awesome Life.

money to be able to allow the unconditional limitless awesome flow of money to come to you.

How you treat money also affects the ability to bring more to you. If your actions are saying you fear having it or frightened of spending it, then you are effectively pushing it away with negative feelings. If you love the fact that having the money means you can let go of it and spend it happily, then more money can come to replace the amount you have spent.

So, you need to take the focus OFF the actual money. Because money does not really exist. It is the ability to be able to trade or buy something from another person and this does not need your attention. The object or service that you want to buy with the money is what makes you excited, happy, fulfilled and gives you pleasure, so that's what you need to put your focus on, – the *FEELING* of having what you want to buy.

Here is a line that hopefully helps you see money in a different way – *Its not your money, it's just your turn.* Think about the journey that coin or paper note has had before it even gets to you. Originally it came from a bank and was given to someone who withdrew it out of their account. It was then passed onto a shopkeeper as that person paid for groceries and then the shopkeeper used it to pay his staff as part of their wages. That member of staff then took that note to the local pub and paid for his drink over the bar. Then you walked in and received it back as change.

Brian's Guide to Manifesting an Awesome Life.

Handing over money for a pair of shoes that bring you *JOY* is easier than paying for a huge electricity bill. But if instead of complaining about the cost of electricity, you instead focus on feeling satisfied and happy that your beautiful home has working lights and appliances making your life comfortable, more money will flow to you. Or the electricity bill will come down and being in the frame of mind of practicing GRATITUDE, you will feel elated when you realise you have more money in your account to buy shoes OR CHEESE!

So, for those of you who have children, help them out a bit and don't let them feel crushed when they want something luxurious or expensive when they grow up. Statements such as "you have to work hard in life" " Money doesn't grow on trees" "You have to earn everything you've got" all help to bring the feeling guilt and resentment toward nice things in life. When your child feels utter elation at the sight of that sports car parked on the neighbours driveway, don't dampen their spirits by revealing your jealousy, envy or utter detest for showoffs. Allow them to enjoy and experience the natural ability to manifest their own insanely happy and awesome life! Maybe, you would be better learning from them, as your way hasn't worked up until now has it?

Brian's Guide to Manifesting an Awesome Life.

The gratitude we spoke about in the last chapter also applies to manifesting money as well as love. Remember the simple rule of the universe, you get more of how you feel about something, so let's learn how to turn your current way of thinking around real fast.

Being able to **FEEL** excitement when you find a penny on the floor or a pound in the supermarket trolley, will tell the universe you absolutely love having money. Hesitating and wondering if you will get into trouble for taking it or focusing on the embarrassment of anyone seeing you take it as it highlights your current financial state , is the fast track to more money problems. Feeling that the penny will not make much difference to your troubles as its nowhere near enough will have the same effect as saying outrightly no thanks to any financial help and you'd rather struggle thanks.

Stop focusing on your financial problem and the fact that you don't YET have enough money for something and start noticing and appreciating the money that you DO have. This is the sure way to allow more money to flow into your life.

Whilst trialling this book on the online course, people's financial situations changed dramatically within a few months, going from broke to a permanent better standard of living. Money began to flow in; unexpected refunds were given from over payments years ago and pay rises came without being asked for. Windfalls and wins ranging from £10 to £10,000 were had and the

Brian's Guide to Manifesting an Awesome Life.

group could not help but feel an overwhelming sense of awe for the way the universe brought the money to each person. They acknowledged and felt thanks for each amount equally regardless of how big or small the amount was.

The way the money arrived to each person was never in a way that could have been predicted. It was never from chasing or asking for a refund, it was never in a way they could have even thought of. It was always a surprise and completely unexpected. Why? (sit yourself down, here comes the lightbulb moment)

BECAUSE THE UNIVERSE WAS BRINGING YOU MORE *JOY*, NOT MORE MONEY.

Re read that until it sinks in guys and gals. The universe responds to your *FEELING* not to your requests and begging and pleading for money. Money does not exist remember. The universe absolutely loves seeing you living your soul/sole purpose in life to the max – which is purely to experience the feeling of the emotion you set as your intention in your root chakra.

So, the right thing to do when this abundance of money arrives in your lap is to spend it on what you need, want, would like and love. If it makes you happy at the thought of having money in a savings account then put it there, but don't deprive yourself of the things you love or need at the same time through fear of running out of money. There is certainly enough money to buy a selection of cheese right now and there is the realization

Brian's Guide to Manifesting an Awesome Life.

that there is an endless supply for you. So, you don't benefit by hiding the money away and not spending it. When that big bill lands on your doorstep and you have the money, pay the bill. Focus on the feeling of gratitude that you can sort it worry free. You are provided for! The next time the tax bill arrives, instead of delaying payment to the last legal day, pay it the moment you can. With ***JOY***! This way more money will come to you freely as the universe sees you love to spend money when needed. The larger amounts of money that you dream of will also flow when you stop withholding large amounts of money going out. So, you can see how saying that something is too expensive is negatively affecting the amount of money coming to you.

So hopefully you now understand how the big house you dream of can come to you as easily as the penny on the floor. Let go of the negativity you associate with money and focus on the feeling of happiness and joy that living in a house that is yours, not somebody else's will bring to you. Feel the excitement of walking around the house and the relief you will feel that you own a beautiful home at long last. When you think of all the reasons you want a bigger house, such as being able to have a room for each of your children or an office so you can work from home comfortably, have fun imagining how easy and wonderful your life will be. See in your mind your children having their own space and feel the utter joy you will experience having an office instead of a corner of the kitchen table to work from.

Brian's Guide to Manifesting an Awesome Life.

What about the fact that there are other people a lot worse off than you that need money for essentials and the basics in life that you have tonnes of? What about the common decency that it is kind to share? Giving is the right thing to do as a good person and sharing what you have is right. Well my answer is this, sharing involves giving to someone else AND looking after yourself. Sharing means, dividing between people, so you must also include your-self. Think of it this way, once you sort out your self-worth and realise you are worthy of receiving abundance, you will have more to share with others! You will be able to help more people, knowing deep down there is more to come to all of you. You could also pass on the understanding of money to ensure you help that other person in huge life changing ways.

Now go enjoy the abundant life you absolutely ***deserve***.

TO DO LIST

Focus on the feeling of satisfaction you will have when you have everything you need and wish for

Get ready for the surprise of how the money will arrive.

Brian's Guide to Manifesting an Awesome Life.

CHAPTER TEN:
The Throat Chakra

The throat chakra when healthy shines the most beautiful angelic blue colour and is responsible for the health of not only your throat but the thyroid gland and the airways to your all-important lungs. Because the thyroid gland controls the hormones, it is a vital chakra to maintain the balance of the entire body, including the heart and brain, even the bones in your bodies support frame. If this chakra is blocked, not only will you experience things like a sore throat or worse, you will also have deep emotional problems that no amount of hormone medication will properly fix. The teeth are also affected by this one, so ongoing dental problems can be resolved by focusing on the emotional needs of this chakra. It is responsible for **Communication**, **Truth** and **Empathy**.

So, what is needed to keep this chakra spinning healthily? *Speaking your truth.*

That sounds easy but I am willing to bet all of you have an issue with this essential chakra. Take a deeper look at your neck area, even noticing the health of the skin on the outside. Is it dry, sore, broken skin? Do you constantly have to clear your throat with a dry tickle? Let's read on and get you healthy.

Brian's Guide to Manifesting an Awesome Life.

Communication and Truth

Voicing how you feel is harder than you think if you are a nice, thoughtful person. Society has told you it's not nice at all to have an opinion about others and its polite to withhold your thoughts and feelings. I am sure you have experienced many times disagreements with others, that made you quite literally shut up and keep your thoughts to yourself from then on.

Well, we have already learnt together how important it is to get *self-ish* for your own health. Now we will learn how crucial it is that you voice your thoughts and feelings. I am not saying that you are to go round telling everybody to their face that you disagree with them and that they irritate you to the core, but I am saying that you need to let those words out at the very least, to yourself.

Stop blocking your truth. Its destroying you.

If your answer to the above was that you do not have any bad thoughts or opinions about anybody in your life, try again, because I don't believe you. I am not asking you to share them with anyone other than your-SELF and you are safe to speak your truth in your own company.

People who have experienced controlling relationships with other humans will find it difficult to

Brian's Guide to Manifesting an Awesome Life.

be able to do this at first, but go ahead, take your time, you are allowed to be true to yourself, including your thoughts.

And for those of you that have trouble containing your anger and are liable to explode with rage at the tiniest of triggers, read on please. This is also for you. You still have a block with this chakra as all you can voice easily is your anger, but you are not telling the truth to yourself. It is the easy option to blame someone else for your misfortune, the hardest thing ever is to get to the core of your anger and piece together why other people can set you off so easily. What are you avoiding? Let's forgive yourself right now and remember that you are a beautiful soul that deserves to be heard and helped.

So, you ready? I want you to make a few lists. You can be as judging as you like here, but I need you to say it out loud as you write it all down.

List 1. People who have pissed you off

This can include the annoying check out lady who threw your fresh vegetables down the conveyer belt carelessly.

The neighbour that plays their music too loudly when you are trying to sleep.

Brian's Guide to Manifesting an Awesome Life.

The person who does not pick up their dog poop on the street outside your house.

The sister who seems to have a better relationship with your parents.

The brother who lives a carefree materialistic life and can't seem to grasp the need for responsibilities.

The ex.

Does it feel good? Is your list getting easier to write as you get started ? It should be. Let it flow. Now for the second list folks.

List 2. People that frustrate you because they won't listen.

Here we might have for example:

The child in your life who should be understanding responsibility by now but is not.

Your parents as they won't let you help them

Your friend that phones for your advice but then does the exact opposite.

Get it all out guys, write their name and the reason why they frustrate the absolute hell out of you.

List 3. People you just do not like. Period.

Brian's Guide to Manifesting an Awesome Life.

This list could include several people and if you let it flow, it may surprise even you who ends up on this list.

It could be:

A person on your social media account.

A celebrity that gets everywhere

A sibling

A parent or relative.

Now take a deep breath and pat yourself on the back, because being a nice all-round polite person, that must have taken some effort. Please don't feel bad if it flowed easily, it simply means you are working perfectly on your-SELF for once. By the way, if you repeatedly had to clear your throat or even burst into a coughing fit, this is a fantastic bit of proof that you have just done some clearing here.

So now we must look at how else you withhold your truth. Common "Lies" that come out of your mouth are:

I am fine

I am happy

Brian's Guide to Manifesting an Awesome Life.

"I am fine" is a great way to stop a person probing into your problems and ending the intrusion. "I am fine" says I don't think this person really wants to know how I'm truly feeling, or, I don't think this person can be trusted with what's really going on, or, I don't think this person has time for me to answer that genuinely. So, you answer politely and quickly and return the polite greeting of asking how they are too.

There's the problem with society these days, the question "How are you?" is used as a greeting the same as hello. People do not wait for an answer as life is so busy for you all.

So personal responsibility kicks in now and going back to what we learnt about becoming your own best friend is crucial. If nobody else is there to ask you how you are, you ask yourself, looking at your reflection in the mirror. Ask yourself how you are truly feeling and be prepared to listen and act on the answer.

To help pull the truth out of your-SELF, I want you to put the palm of your hand hovering over, not touching, the middle of your throat. Sit quietly for a moment and open up to receive the divine light from up above and draw it down through your head, feeling it flow through your skull, neck, shoulders, arms, fingertips, spine, chest, tummy, hips, legs, knees, shins and feet. Repeat a few times keeping your hand hovering over the throat.

Brian's Guide to Manifesting an Awesome Life.

Now push the energy that is pouring out of the palm of your hand into the throat chakra and say out loud the words:

I AM

Repeat the simple words, feeling the beautiful golden energy flow clearing your throat over and over until an emotion or word follows. It will be something like….

I AM ANGRY

I AM SCARED

I AM FRIGHTENED

I AM LONELY

Please do not hold back on the emotion you are feeling as you connect with the right word. If you need to cry, then cry. If you feel like shouting, then let the anger out. Keep your hand hovering over the throat and draw more of that divine energy. Allow your true voice to speak as you continue the sentence. Now you have the emotion, you will be able to speak the reason, so do not hold anything back.

I AM ANGRY BECAUSE MY EX PARTNER…….

I AM SCARED BECAUSE I DON'T THINK I CAN….

Brian's Guide to Manifesting an Awesome Life.

    I AM FRIGHTENED BECAUSE I MIGHT GET HURT IF I LOVE AGAIN….

    I AM LONELY BUT CAN'T LET ANYONE IN.

    We don't need solutions; we just need your truth to come out. That is all I ask you to do at this stage. Let the weight of the truth leave your body, it always feels better, and you will feel physically lighter after releasing your fears.

    Now go back to where we learnt with the solar plexus that connects you to the universe, that you have all the help on hand when you allow it to come in and finally accept the help. The universe and its helpers in the form of your guides have been waiting for this moment, when you can truly let them in.

    Now is the time to ask them to help you with the worries and burdens you have voiced.

    Keeping the hand over the throat and allowing the light to flow in, tell the universe truthfully what your soul wants without the fear or preempting the solutions or conditioning the answer. Remember too, you are only in control of yourself, not another human being.

    I WANT TO BE LOVED

    I WANT TO QUIT MY JOB

Brian's Guide to Manifesting an Awesome Life.

I WANT TO CHANGE CAREERS

Feel the love flow to you, feel in your gut that you have connected and been heard, now you have spoken your truth. That is all you had to do, to allow the help to flood in. Feel yourself connected to the higher self and breathe with a sense of relief that help is here. Instantly.

Empathy

Empathy is the word to describe being able to feel and share other people's feelings. You may hear people declare themselves as an empath. The truth is everyone is, as it is in you as a human being to be able to feel compassion and understanding for others. When you truly have compassion, you are able to use all your senses including being able to physically feel and put yourself in their shoes, while understanding their point of view or way of looking at a situation. It's an awesome way of helping another person and stopping yourself from being judgmental and taking it personally.

Continuing with the process of drawing the light through the top of your head, flowing all the way through your entire body, fill the stomach with the light and now breathe with your stomach inflating and deflating properly with each breath. As the sacral chakra

Brian's Guide to Manifesting an Awesome Life.

in your tummy is filled with the divine energy you are drawing in, you will begin to feel compassion for all the people or situations that helped to create your initial anger and blocks. Being able to have true compassion means understanding someone else's side of things and being able to see where they were coming from. It allows you to feel with true passion the emotion they were working through when at first you only reacted to their action or words aimed at you. You can now understand that it was not actually aimed at you, they were projecting their own fear and negative emotions and you fell in the firing line.

    You can now stop taking it personally. This does not mean you have to do anything else but understand. You do NOT put up with someone's attacks and hate, you are allowed to walk away and preserve your own wellbeing, but now as you walk away, you send them the same love and divine energy from the universe that has made such an awesome difference to your wellbeing. And now you can hope that they find the same success as you.

    All the hard work you have done so far is beginning to pay off. Having a sense of self-worth is vital and today you have managed to get out the feelings that were literally stuck in your throat and allowed your true voice to be heard.

    When another soul says or does something that irritates you, you can now stick up for yourself and say

Brian's Guide to Manifesting an Awesome Life.

no. You can now voice confidently how you feel in order to be your new best friend and protect him or her from unnecessary harm.

The way you speak **of** yourself will now be positive and you can speak **for** yourself positively too.

I AM WORTHY OF HAPPINESS

I AM EXCITED TO HAVE HAPPINESS

I AM GUIDED BY THE UNIVERSE

I AM ENOUGH

I AM WORTHY

After clearing the throat chakra in this way, you will be able to voice your needs much more easily to other human beings too. When someone asks if they can help you in anyway and tells you to shout if you need them, now you can! If the answer is no from someone and you find it was a hollow offer out of politeness, you won't feel anger, you will accept the answer. You won't take it personally, instead you will find another person to help, whereas before you would have shut down and assumed you were not worthy of another person's help. When someone asks you how you are, you will either be able to answer honestly, or find that you don't need that person to help you as in fact, you have found the way of accepting the awesome help of the universe and you are

Brian's Guide to Manifesting an Awesome Life.

self-sufficient, being able to cope without telling all your problems to others.

Being able to stand up for yourself also means fear will no longer control the way you speak up or refrain from speaking at all. You will find the courage to stand alone and not feel the need to join in when others judge another person or situation. You will no longer have the worry that if you do not do or say as another human wants you to, to validate their point of view, you will suffer. You can now see that you can have your own opinion and feel confident in standing alone. You will find peace in your personal power.

The realisation that your body is so much more than just a physical body, but rather it houses all the tools to assist you emotionally too can be mind blowing. What an incredible creation you are!

Please shout your needs confidently whenever you require help from the universe and your guides. Ask for help with anything and everything. It can be help with ensuring a parking space is available right outside the office door, to help with bringing the right amount of money in to pay a bill. It's all the same to the universe, a request by you to help you fulfill your life purpose. Your little secretary stood beside you is waiting with a pen and paper, to write down all that you would like him to do.

Brian's Guide to Manifesting an Awesome Life.

By the way, this is such an important chakra to keep healthy for anyone that works as a psychic helping others with guidance from the universe. The words you pass on as messages may come out of your mouth, but they are direct from the universe and your guide if you are channeling properly. This means the throat chakra must be clear in order to prevent you from stalling, affecting or even changing the message you've been trusted to pass on, through your own fear or need to control. If you have an ounce of doubt or fear of the message, you are acting as if it is coming from you. If you acknowledge and trust that you are just the channel for the message to be passed through, you let go of all responsibility and pass it on exactly as it was intended from your guide.

Woohoo! May I say how utterly proud of you I am today? I think it is the perfect time to reward that new best friend of yours with something that brings them the emotion you set as your intention right at the beginning of this book. Go eat that cheese. Handfuls of it!

Brian's Guide to Manifesting an Awesome Life.

TO DO LIST

Check in on yourself regularly and ask how you are truly feeling privately.

Ask for help from the universe.

Practice strengthening your empathy for helping to understand another person's behaviour

Brian's Guide to Manifesting an Awesome Life.

CHAPTER ELEVEN:

The Third Eye Chakra

So here we have the chakra that everybody associates with the ability to be "psychic" and clairvoyant. Hopefully by now, you can already see that the whole body needs to be used as a pure channel for the divine energy of the universe to function fully, and not just this one chakra. You may already see that it's not just a chosen few who have the ability to work with guides or the universe, as it is in fact a human ability. There is no such thing as a carefully selected, more capable gifted person. The only difference is the human being who uses all their senses and entire human body as a channel for the universe will be able to connect with the universe perfectly, and the one who works through fear or half of their true capability will not.

The online course that this book is based on, was also used by amazing psychics, still searching for their inner happiness. They, just like everyone else suffered with anxiety, depression and were not living an incredibly awesome life. They had blocks with money and love just like everyone else. Yet, they knew how to work with the third eye chakra and did so daily in order to help others. As we have already covered so far in this book, seeing your self-worth and acknowledging that you are just as important as everyone else in your life is

Brian's Guide to Manifesting an Awesome Life.

vital. You will find that clairvoyants and psychics who have not sorted their stuff out, are the kindest people, wanting to help everyone else before themselves, but why is this? The answer to that my friend is that they have battled so much with their own fears and insecurities, they somewhere along the line decided it was much easier to focus on helping and loving anybody else other than themselves. They also have to put up with judgement from people about what they do for a living as it is still very much misunderstood and feared by many.

The third eye chakra when spinning healthily affects the wellbeing and healthy function of the eyes, ears, sinuses and the front part of the brain. It is the most divine purple or mauve colour. It is such an important one as you can already see. If you have constant sinusitis, headaches and migraines, this chakra needs your full attention. It is worth noting now that scientifically, the front part of the brain called the frontal lobe, is responsible for your ability to problem solve, memory, language and judgement in a situation. It is known as the control panel for your entire body. So, a blocked third eye chakra, can cause a whole array of physical problems, right down to struggling to think and remember things. It is responsible for your **knowledge** and **intuition**.

The most common problem that blocks this chakra is fear and anxiety, stemming from the thought of being alone and the only one responsible for controlling

Brian's Guide to Manifesting an Awesome Life.

things. Shutting down as a channel and dealing with life by yourself is exhausting!

So, what are you frightened of, if your third eye worked perfectly? Could it be that you are fearful of what you may see with your third eye? You know full well that you are able to see evidence of a bigger world around if this chakra works well, so is it a fear of seeing spirit that holds you back? Or is it a particular person that you don't know how to react to if you were able to see them?

Ask yourself truthfully, is the fear a fear of having to experience all the heartache and sadness again, if you were able to see the one you lost. The lady who we all know a little too well now in my life, had her heart literally shattered into pieces when her husband and father to her children died of cancer. She works as a channel daily to allow me to speak through her to help others and she is fully aware of all the souls that have passed having a sneaky peak in to see if they can have a chat too. She knows damn well her husband is right next to her every step of the day, but doing exactly as she is saying, which is to back off as she hasn't got time for another breakdown. In order to survive, she has built up a wall of protection, so she doesn't collapse. If she saw him peer over her shoulder as she is typing right now for me, she wouldn't be able to keep writing. If she took note of the cheeky smile and allowed herself to notice the way he was resting his chin on her shoulder, with the smell of his Paul Smith aftershave wafting up her nose,

Brian's Guide to Manifesting an Awesome Life.

the crushing overwhelming pain of loss would envelop her and she would not be able to compose herself. The day would be written off as she would have to focus on the work she needs to do to forgive herself that she couldn't save him or help as he died in her arms.

For the record, there is no time in spirit. No clocks and no deadline, excuse the pun. You can take years if you need, their spirit or soul will always be there when you are ready to talk.

What if there is a person that made your life absolute utter hell when they were in your life, and now they have passed over, you are terrified of them being able to come back into your world again? Or you are glad they aren't around anymore and deep down worried as to how they might feel if there was a way they would know. I want you to remember when we talked earlier in this book about every other living soul being on a learning journey about emotions the same as you. Remember that they too, had lessons to learn and were worthy of forgiveness and love just the same as everyone else. Forgiving them and wishing them well on their never-ending journey through the universe and time and many different lives, is vital for your own personal health and happiness.

When a soul leaves the body and gets to the other side they are no longer restricted by human emotional blocks. The same emotional blocks that you are working on to improve right now. So, if they were living a life of anger,

Brian's Guide to Manifesting an Awesome Life.

resentment and blame without personal responsibility, they will now be free of those emotions in spirit. Unconditional love greeted them when they left their body and the ability to see the bigger picture was healing for them. It is the reality of what you are all trying to achieve here on earth, inner peace and understanding – LOVE. So, they are not looking on at you through human eyes, even your biggest enemy that has passed on, will be looking at you with love, compassion and a true desire to see you achieve your dreams.

Some of these souls may if you let them, want to show you their love and make peace with you. They may appear trying to help and give you assistance if you let them. They may just want to ask for your forgiveness, as they recognize how their actions affected you. This decision is up to you, you don't have to and you won't offend anyone if you say no (hopefully you can now see that it doesn't matter if you do offend anyone, it's you and you only that matters here).

However, there is a difference between a soul that was once a human being giving you advice and your guide. The personal helper assigned to helping you by the universe is the one who will guide you in the right direction even when you resist. Your guide will help you overcome your internal battles and help you take new steps forward even when you may feel unable to. They will guide you with the truth, not what makes you feel better. Your loved ones that have passed over, will be supporting you with loving words of support, and try and

Brian's Guide to Manifesting an Awesome Life.

prove to you that they still exist, in order to give you the peace of knowing that you don't have to worry about them. But please, when it comes to taking guidance and direction from spirit, only work with your guide. Would you take advice from your sweet old gran about where to invest your savings or which car to buy? Stick with your guides, they will tell you like it is.

KNOWLEDGE

When working healthily, the third eye chakra allows you to process the information you are receiving when connected to the divine flow of energy up above. When you are an open channel and accepting that the guidance comes from above for every single situation you experience in life, you will find you receive solutions and just know the answers instantly. Nothing feels like a problem anymore as the solution is "shown" to you. Just simply not trying to control everything and allowing the free-flowing love of the universe up above your head brings answers to you. Remember the part where we talked earlier in the root chakra chapter, about stopping stressing over something that you can't control and instead focusing on something creative that brings you pleasure or *JOY*, if even for a moment. So whilst gardening, drawing, cooking, singing or even eating the biggest block of cheese you can find in the fridge, you are taking the pressure off the third eye chakra and the answers can flow freely to you, whilst you're preoccupied.

Brian's Guide to Manifesting an Awesome Life.

This is where you get the lightbulb moment out of nowhere. The idea, the answer, completely stress free and without effort. You will sense and know it is right by using the solar plexus chakra that we have unblocked and become guided by how you *FEEL*.

INTUITION

The need for many of you to know who your guide is, is understandable, yet not necessary. If you have removed the blocks so far in your other chakras, you will now be working with trust, faith and knowing. The utter joy that you feel connecting with the universe and its helpers is all you need to be able to see them without fear. There are many ways to help strengthen the third eye in order to physically see the world around you in spirit form, such as meditation.

The woman in my life who we all know far too well now, has written a book for me once before called Brian's Guide to Working with Spirit, which contains a few meditations you may like. They are also available on her YouTube channel. Just type in Rhiannon Faulkner in YouTube and you will find them there for free. Meditation is also extremely beneficial to the entire body as it relaxes and centers you. Just the simple process of connecting to the divine guidance from above and sitting still within your own energy is grounding and calming. Meditation will leave you feeling refreshed and brighter every time.

Brian's Guide to Manifesting an Awesome Life.

The simple exercise of staring ahead and seeing how far to each side of the room you are able to see without moving your head, strengthens the ability to use your third eye, instead of your physical pair of eyes. I am sure you have all been in the position where out of nowhere you sense or see something unusual in the corner of your eye. You turn quickly, to point your human eyes and its gone. Stop using your human eyes and it will work. So, next time you sense something out of your line of vision, keep looking in the same direction as you already are, but breathe calmly, and extend your peripheral vision instead. Whatever or whoever it was will still be there. Now you can also extend that peripheral vision to seeing what's behind you without turning around. After enough practice, being able to take the focus off your human eyes and solely using your spiritual one instead will become natural.

Another simple exercise is to close your eyes and say what you see. People will proclaim that they see nothing, and it is just black. But that is when you are only using your human physical eyes. If you relax and take in all that is happening, you may begin to see a lighter shade of black appear, or swirls of grey, and flickers of light. Small dots of white or bright yellow appear like a fuzzy tv screen from the olden days. As you relax more, people, blue, green colours in white space the colours swirl and move across in front of you, taking the form of recognizable shapes. It could be butterflies, balloons, faces. Continue going with the flow, and recognising

Brian's Guide to Manifesting an Awesome Life.

what you see or what the colours and shapes remind you of. The moment you dismiss something, you switch off and shut down. Reopen the top of your head and draw down to the divine energy free flowing through you and let all your thoughts flow freely too. You will find yourself thinking of people, scenes and before you know it, you will be in full "imagination" flow and watching a film in your minds eye.

Now imagination is important to be able to *"see"* spirit and it is already a human ability that you were born with, but over time you have shut down. But not completely, because when you read a book, or someone tells you a story, you are able to quite literally see what they are talking about. The frustration people feel when they want to be able to see spirit leads to an utter obsession with wanting to see them in 3d form and just like a physical person. The answer to this is you already can! When you read typed words in a book, flat on a page in black and white, your brain can translate that into real life images and pictures in your mind's eye. That is the third eye – your "mind's eye". This is how you are already able to see spirit around you. It starts with imagination and then adding in all your other abilities as a human channel such as empathy, compassion, and knowing, coupled with your clear throat chakra, you are able to speak without fear, you can now even pass on the guidance from above to others ! The whole body with all chakras working together give you the desired ability to be "psychic".

Brian's Guide to Manifesting an Awesome Life.

But having a healthy third eye chakra isn't just to help you see spirit. The visions can help with practical things to improve your daily life. When living a busy life and trying to remember all that you need to do, it is a hard task if you attempt it alone. If you allow the universe in and accept the help using this chakra to its full potential, life will be a lot easier. So, when you have ten things to do before midday, receiving the vision and knowledge of the best way to tackle a problem really makes a difference in being able to get everything done.

Remember the front of the brain that controls memory is affected by this chakra, and a stressed and overloaded brain is not helpful to anyone. Writing lists and using post it notes to remind yourself of things to do is a good way to help you in difficult times. Writing lists and post it notes for your GUIDE is a great way to help you remember that you have already asked them to help in certain ways. This isn't for the benefit of your guide or the universe because they don't need reminding twice, but do you recall what we said about doubt in previous chapters? Asking over and over for help is telling the universe that you doubt they're going to help, so the universe hears doubt and unworthiness from you. Ask once, write it down and stick it somewhere you can confidently see what your guide is already getting on with for you. This will also build up the trust between the two of you, bring you more time to get on with your

Brian's Guide to Manifesting an Awesome Life.

soul/sole purpose in life – finding the fun and *JOY* in everything you do.

The hearing is also controlled by this amazing chakra and the ability to hear your guide is another essential, yet normal human ability, that has been lost over the years. The same as with the eyes, it is not actually the human ears on the side of the head that you use to hear them, the "spiritual" ears are located slightly lower on the side of the face.

To be able to get used to using them, there are a couple of great ways to practice.

You are all able to hold a conversation with yourselves inside your head. You can ask yourself a question and answer yourself immediately without using your vocal cords. When you are speaking to your guide, you will hear the answer to your question before you've even finished asking the question. That is the simplest way of explaining it to you. Go ahead, practice now. Don't forget to open up and connect to that divine energy free flowing above your headfirst. Then ask any question, your guide is right behind you waiting to join in the fun, rather looking forward to connecting with you in such a personal way.

The other way of getting used to using your spiritual ears, is again connecting and drawing down the divine energy from above and just letting it flow over

Brian's Guide to Manifesting an Awesome Life.

and over through your entire body down to the feet and then focusing on the flow coming out of your head and through your ear canal on both sides. Repeat this, focusing on the **FEEL** of the light as it goes through your ears. You will experience a strange sound or crackling as the connection is made. It may sound like an echo or radio channel being tuned trying to get the right frequency. Just go with it until you are aware of how far you can actually hear sounds now. You are clearing your ears out and not a cotton bud in sight!

    The voice may sound like yours but a little deeper when you begin to connect, but as long as the answer to your question comes before you've even finished your question, you know its your guide. Have fun getting to know each other, this is quite literally your "soul mate". Don't be surprised when after a while of being able to chat away to each other, you hear humour and pure wit in their answers. Maybe a little sarcasm. The universe doesn't do stroppiness or moods, it is full of unconditional love and pure **JOY**. Fun laughter and humour is all part of the high vibration you will be working on. **EN-JOY** – LIFE IS GOOD!

Brian's Guide to Manifesting an Awesome Life.

A common way for people to react when they receive clear guidance and have a vision of something about to happen in the near future, is to control it. So, let's take as an example, you have heard, seen and felt that you will be finding love soon and become blissfully happy. You may have even had details such as a description of what the person looks like or does for a living. Instead of feeling gratitude and excitement for what's coming up, some people become obsessed and put all their energy into trying to make that vision or prediction true. That's the moment it is ruined as you are instantly blocking the universe from being able to bring it to you. Let go and let the magic come to you. The message given to you was meant to reassure you, not to make you panic or to tell you that you must create it. It has already been created! Its on its way! Please for the love of cheese, put it to the back of your mind and ***en-JOY*** the journey. If you search for this person coming into your life, you may change the path they were about to enter. If you were meant to meet in a particular place that the universe had divinely timed, you may be off searching in completely the wrong place or worse, you may have forced it so much , you end up with a different person, who fits half the description!

Brian's Guide to Manifesting an Awesome Life.

Just let go and let it come to you naturally, trust that the universe and your guides know exactly how to bring you the end result, and you just keep telling them and showing you what brings you utter JOY and HAPPINESS.

TO DO LIST

Meditate

Practice strengthening the third eye with exercises

Brian's Guide to Manifesting an Awesome Life.

CHAPTER TWELVE:
The Crown Chakra

The crown chakra is the final one we must unblock, and it is located slightly above the top of your head. When healthy, it shines a beautiful pure white colour and allows you to receive the **guidance** and see the true **potential** in a situation. It affects the health of your mind and physical brain, so you can see in order to be in a healthy state of mind, we need to suss this baby out.

Physical symptoms that show this chakra may need some help are headaches, panic attacks, depression, hair loss and sore scalp.

Throughout this book, I have asked you to connect to the divine glorious universe by opening up the top of your head and allowing the light in. A great way to physically feel this chakra begin to work is a trapdoor opening up in your skull, or a sliding door, opening fully. The traditional way is to imagine a lotus flower opening up all its petals sitting on your head. Whatever works for you is the one that you go with, but please, let your imagination run wild here.

As you focus on doing this, you will be able to feel a pressure, or tingling around the top half of your head as it begins to work. As you draw the energy down

Brian's Guide to Manifesting an Awesome Life.

through your body, the feeling of warmth, comfort and safety will rush through every tiny part of your body.

Please notice how your physical pain actually disappears every single time you do this and your fears, anxiety and feelings of being inadequate leave so quickly too. What IS that powerful stuff that you've allowed into your body and how the actual heck can it have such an immediate, positive healing effect?

It is ***LOVE***.

Yes, you are feeling the physical effect of ***receiving love.*** The same love that you have deprived yourself of having by self-loathing, by believing that you didn't deserve to be loved, by giving your power to a person or situation that once made you think you weren't worthy of being loved.

So, the instant feeling of physical health and wellbeing, coupled with ***hope, passion*** and ***JOY*** for life can be achieved by opening and connecting to the free-flowing LOVE the universe has for you.

Try shutting down and cutting off the supply really quickly. Shut the trap door, or close down the lotus flower. You will instantly feel cold inside, like the temperature has dropped and every physical pain you live with will be back again. The tight chest, the sore arthritic knee, the dodgy shoulder.... So, if every physical pain stems from an emotional problem, this means that because you are not connected to the

Brian's Guide to Manifesting an Awesome Life.

universe, your blocks of negative thoughts toward yourself are back.

Open up again before you read on, there is no need to sit there and suffer for another moment in your life.

It can even be an incredibly emotional experience letting love into your mind,body and soul. It feels like coming home, being complete, being enough. In fact, it feels just like how good it feels when you are IN LOVE with another human being at the start of a relationship. That's because it's the same magic – LOVE.

The lightbulb moment of realising that the universe has been trying to LOVE you the whole time you have been alive is a bit of a big one. You can hopefully now see that everything you have been searching for from another human being has been available to you UNCONDITIONALLY from the universe.

When you *FEEL* how absolutely awesome it feels to RECEIVE love just like you've been dishing out to every single person you care about, you can see why it has been so detrimental to your physical and emotional health and you may just be able to understand why you've had a hard time of it up until now.

It is natural for you to want to know more and understand what or where it is coming from. Because the simple word LOVE seems just that, too simple. Society

Brian's Guide to Manifesting an Awesome Life.

has tried to control your **personal power** by bringing religion into the equation and beliefs that continue down family lines for generations. Pressure has been put onto you by schools, families, groups, churches, countries and people you go to for advice. Churches and even some families rule with fear, stating that if you do not conform, you are a bad person and will suffer in an afterlife if you do not follow their ways. Even if you are strong enough to shun them, the little tiny feeling of doubt is left inside you at times.

Cut the ties that you have had in place and stay open to the unconditional love that is available to you from the universe.

Let's understand and have COMPASSION for the followers of groups, societies and religions. They are trying to do the right thing and be a good person. They are searching for the *sense of belonging* and *purpose* that you have just found by finding your *personal power*. There is no need for you to judge anyone when you have compassion and understanding.

What matters here is YOU. Do you feel good when connecting to the LOVE that is freely available to you from the universe? Does it make you feel healthy, happy, excited and confident? Then keep letting the love in for you, as well as giving it to all the people you care for. Include yourself in the pecking order and you will have more love to give to the others. You will be healthy

Brian's Guide to Manifesting an Awesome Life.

enough to live a full vibrant inspiring life and seeing your self-worth.

GUIDANCE AND POTENTIAL

Not only does the crown chakra bring you the love that you need in your life, but it is also the place where the **guidance** comes. This is where it enters your body and with the use of all the other chakras or energy centers in your body, you process the guidance, **see**, **feel** and **act** on it.

Your whole body becomes a pure channel or tube for the love to flow through and allows each vital chakra to spin healthily and work to its true potential.

The guidance comes to you as thoughts and ideas. This is where you suddenly think of a solution to a problem or get the answer to something you have been wanting to achieve, or a way to move forward on your path to achieving your goals.

Just allow the ideas to flow now and continue to feel the excitement and gratitude. If logic kicks in and you find yourself questioning how to even begin making the idea work, then you have shut down by trying to control the outcome. You are preferring to keep the problem rather than solving it. This is the same old streak of fear that has prevented you from going for your goals in the past, so re connect, busy yourself with something that brings you pure JOY and let the guidance continue.

Brian's Guide to Manifesting an Awesome Life.

Remember, you get what you give your energy to, so if you're sitting there saying, hmmm great idea but it would never work, as I can foresee this problem and that obstacle, you've just told the universe that you don't need help as you like to create problems.

If you go with the flow of **FEELING JOY** and **HAPPINESS**, more guidance will come, to show you every tiny detail of what you need to do next.

The true **potential** of a goal or idea that you have begun to manifest with all the hard work you've done on your root chakra, is beginning to be seen. This is when you get your proof that your manifesting has worked, and the universe has heard you and already been acting on your request.

So, things around you are going to change and fast. The universe is working with your intentions and being **RIDICULOUSLY POSITIVE** has paid off!

People will leave your life if they are holding you back, new faces will come to join you in your life who will be a part of your new way of living. If you have manifested a new house, then the way you work will have to change too, in order to bring the financial abundance to you. Don't fight the change, instead clear each fear or block that you feel as you go along head-on. Go back to the beginning of this book or flick through and see where you need to focus on to clear your negative thinking.

Brian's Guide to Manifesting an Awesome Life.

Change is good, change is essential, in order to bring everything, you want into your life. It is in-fact a sign of your progress.

What if someone else comes to you with their absolutely crazy idea or goal they would like to achieve and asks you for your opinion or advice? Please, do one thing before you open your mouth or even have your own opinion. Open up and connect, draw down the *LOVE* and channel the guidance you give, to ensure it is positive and coming from a place of truth, not your fear.

I am sure you have experienced being on the receiving end of someone's advice that left you deflated and upset and made you question your sanity as they listed off the practical, sometimes negative reasons why you have lost the plot and your idea won't work. Channeling ensures your own personal views built on negative emotions won't come into the equation and you will have been a positive influence in the person's life. It also gives you the validation that you are okay and doing well in life, without the need to get reassurance from another human being. You have everything you need from the love you can channel to help, support and spur you on.

The moment you feel drained, is the moment the guidance has stopped, and you are actually now trying to hear more, when everything has been said or shown to you that is needed. The questioning has now begun, and doubt has crept in. The need for validating the guidance

Brian's Guide to Manifesting an Awesome Life.

means you do not believe or trust. Busy yourself with something that feels good to keep you in the here and now and full of *JOY*. Its time for that cheese again folks!

TO DO LIST

Open up and let the LOVE in!

Brian's Guide to Manifesting an Awesome Life.

CHAPTER THIRTEEN: Karma

It pains me to see people use karma as a way to wish punishment on someone, because 1. Its not a nice way to treat your fellow earthlings and 2. They are stopping the flow of unconditional love from the universe blessing their life.

Please don't see karma as a punishment, yes you have all heard the phrase, what goes around comes around, but there is more to it than that. Karma is the simple fact that you get what you think of, regarding others. So, if you have treated someone kindly it flows back to you and if you have not, then that flows back to you.

It is a wonderful way to help you understand the all-important compassion you can feel for others from the sacral chakra. The rule of karma says that you will learn to **FEEL** another person's point of view, to be able to help you grow. It's not about their lesson, it is always about yours. So, there is no punishment for your bad behaviour from the universe, only a helping hand in fully feeling how your actions made the other person feel. Likewise, when you have made someone feel great, you will **FEEL** how you made them feel too. All the hard work you have done on yourself through the course of reading this book has been based on the knowing that the universe responds to what you are **FEELING**, so if you are getting satisfaction out of knowing or hoping that someone damn well suffers the way they made you

Brian's Guide to Manifesting an Awesome Life.

suffer, then guess what you're gonna get come your way? Everything you accidentally wished for!

Eventually, you will become aware of how quickly things come round to you and will acknowledge what's happening. When out of nowhere someone is rude to you, like a stranger in a supermarket for example, take the time to think of what you can learn from this. Can you recall when maybe there was a time that you have been rude unintentionally to a stranger in the same situation? Once you can be honest with yourself and see that you too are capable of the same without realising, you will not feel the need to react angrily, or take it personally.

The woman we all know a little too well in my life, when teaching this lesson during the online course for this book, asked at the end, for the universe to help her see what "karmic" lesson she still needed to learn. On the school run that afternoon, she stopped off at the pet shop to buy some treats for her dogs. She parked up, jumped out the car, span round and locked it remotely and lost her balance. (She is getting on a bit now you know, nearly 50 at the time of writing) She gathered her senses and crossed the car park just as another lady was driving by and nearly ran her over. Mrs. F jumped back and raised her hand to wave to say sorry, only to find the driver was not impressed. In-fact, she was fuming and began to shout at her from behind the wheel. As she

Brian's Guide to Manifesting an Awesome Life.

buried her head in shame, Mrs. F quickened her step and went into the pet store, feeling guilty.

She quickly clued on and began to giggle to herself as she realised that her karmic lesson had arrived already for the day. She admitted whole heartedly that she was a quite often a careless driver herself and had been in the drivers seat many a time when she had to slam the brakes on in a car park, for a pedestrian to pass safely. As she crossed the car park to get back to her car, the same thing happened with a different driver and by now she was smiling, reassuring the driver that she was incredibly sorry, stepped back and let them drive past. She cursed me that time if I remember rightly but had accepted fully that her driving was one way that she could become a nicer, more caring person to people around her. Happy to announce she is a more thoughtful driver now and does not get angry or take it personally when people make her slow down to let them pass.

To be able to analyse your reaction to someone else's action, and associate it with a time in your life where you would have had the same feeling, clears up old wounds and gives you a true sense of peace and the ability to not take everything personally. It will also speed up the learning process for you, meaning an easier life!

CHAPTER FOURTEEN:
AND FINALLY......

I hope you can now see after completing the entire book in order, that you were born with all the tools and abilities you need to enjoy a happy, awesome incredible life. I hope you now **FEEL** that you are not alone ever and that the universe is your biggest fan, willing you to feel the emotion that you set as your intention right at the beginning of this journey.

My wish for you is that you realise your own true potential and personal power in each breath that you take moving forward and I hope that you never ever let another human being rule you with fear. May you see your true self as your best friend forever and realise that what you have learnt is a new way of life, not just a short-term change.

Keep taking your best friend on daily short walks and check for depressive fog that has built up around you through fear or negative beliefs. Those little devils can creep in when you are least expecting it. Ask your guide to strip that $%^* away and dispose of it for you.

Brian's Guide to Manifesting an Awesome Life.

    Constantly assess the signs your body is giving you by the colours you are drawn to wearing and the food you suddenly crave. See your body as your temple and treat it with respect, ensuring other people do too.

    Use compassion and empathy wherever you go, understanding that other people's reactions and actions toward you are really nothing to do with you, but that they are growing as a soul themselves, learning along the way. However, do not be afraid to tell them no, as they take a while getting used to your new standards and boundaries! Three strikes and out I say, once and you politely tell them it is not okay to treat you like that anymore, second time, hand out a warning and third, kick that door shut as they leave.

    You are in control of your destiny and the universe is here to help you achieve your wildest dreams. Now you are able to voice your truth, you can manifest literally anything your heart desires, by connecting to the divine source which as we have found out is pure unconditional love that you have deprived yourself of for too long.

    Be prepared for huge changes in life. You asked for change so now you will begin to see new opportunities arise in all areas of your life. We cannot make you take them, so you must continue to trust and go with the flow, removing your blocks as they naturally arrive, through fear. Realigning yourself every step of

Brian's Guide to Manifesting an Awesome Life.

the way is now essential to keep yourself open to receive all the abundance coming to you in all areas of your life.

    Keep removing the limits that you find yourself resetting and acknowledge every single thing that brings you the emotion you set in your root chakra; from the taste of the cheese, to the penny on the floor, from the new shoes on your feet, to the car you drive, from the smile on your loved ones face, to the bank balance that makes you smile.

    Keep **_en-JOY-ing_** your life and see that life is good, when you let the love in, not just out.

    I love you, do you?

    Brian x

Brian's Guide to Manifesting an Awesome Life.

Acknowledgments

A massive shout out and thankyou to every single person that put their trust in us and joined the online course. It's thanks to you, that now I can help more folk with Mrs. F writing this book for me. You helped me help her too personally, something I have been trying to do since the day she lost her husband 11 years ago. By being able to speak through her to you guys, she received the love too. She has now found her sense of belonging and purpose in life and although it took a lot of tears, pain and cheese, she, like you, finally allowed the unconditional love of the universe in.

The support and friendship gained within the group will last a life-time and validate the inner strength you all have, to continue manifesting the most awesome life you can dream of, because you now know you are worthy of having it. As more people join you, I look forward to seeing you all become channels of pure JOY, helping others to find peace and love in their lives.

Love Brian x

Brian's Guide to Manifesting an Awesome Life.

Errrrr, stop reading, you've come to the end. You should be off out manifesting your dreams…. :)

Printed in Great Britain
by Amazon